I0408723

Hinds
&
Woodbury

Family Reunions and Genealogy

Randall Lyon

Contents

Past Reunions

The following pages contain pictures and handouts from previous family reunions. This is by no means a complete history. It is just a quick snapshot of what I was able to gather for this first edition.

It is my hope that this book and the 2017 reunion will help open the door to gathering more photos of family members, history and documentation that can be included in future editions.

Woodbury

Reunion

1991

ANNA ELIZA CORNWELL
9-15-1875-- 2-19-1??

JOHN ELMER WOODBURY
9-27-1870-- 2-11-1943

" THE WOODBURY'S"

John and Anna married , June 5, 1891 , in Palmyria , MI. of this marriage
came eleven children. John was a hard working, kind and very gentle man, with
great love of his family. Anna was a mid-wife, who brought many children of
the family into the world. She cated for the sick, and sat up at many funerals
in the old days.

During the depression, there were family dances , all of the family would
get together and play music and dance, there were the Woodburys, Cousinos,Butlers,
Goutz, Gee,s Hinds, Esenbaugh, Shannaway, Spanglers, Rahm and so many more. Everyone
was welcome in their home.

John and Anna were married almost 48 years when John passed away in 1943.,It was
a marriage of love and caring not only each other and their family, but anyone
who came into their lives.

This book of the Woodbury's, is our past- present - and future of our family,
let us all work to make it a close , happy and proud family.

WOODBURY REUNION 1991

ANNA WOODBURY

John Woodbury

Toledo, Ohio **FEB 2 1 1958**

scrapbooks inc., so. plainfield, n. j.

In Memoriam

JOHNSON—ANNE E. WOODBURY, age 82, of 5612 Yarmouth Dr., mother of Cecil Woodbury, Mrs. Luella Hinds, and Mrs. Nela Rahm, all of Toledo, Herman and Charles Woodbury, Cocoa, Fla., Harry Woodbury and Mrs. Maude Green, both of Monroe, Mich., Mrs. Iva Gard, Salerno, Fla., and Mrs. Laura Hinds, Naples, Fla.; sister of Sylvester Cornwell, Toledo, halfsister of Raymond McDonald, San Francisco, Calif., and Floyd Harrington, Mobile, Ala. Friends may call at the H. H. Birkenkamp Funeral Home, 3219 Tremainsville Rd., Trilby, O. Services Saturday, Feb. 22 at 1:30 p.m. Interment Roselawn Cemetery, Monroe, Mich. CH 3-2183, GR 9-53.

THIS CERTIFIES

That on the Sixth day of
June in the year 189

John H. Woodbury
and
Anne E. Cornell
were by me united in

MARRIAGE

THE WOODBURY FAMILY

(BACK ROW)   LOUIE& MARY   LAURA& NOLA
             SHANNAWAY   WOODBURY

(2nd. ROW)   JESSIE   JUNE   ALVIN   DORTHY
             SHANNAWAY   WOODBURY WOODBURY   HOUCK

(FRONT ROW) ROBERT   CLARENCE   HOWARD
              WOODBURY

ANNA WOOODBURY

1953

WOODBURY GIRLS

NOLA MAUDE LVA LUELLA

NOLA &LAURA

NOLA *LUELLA* LAURA
1927

NOLA* LAURA* LUELLA
1927

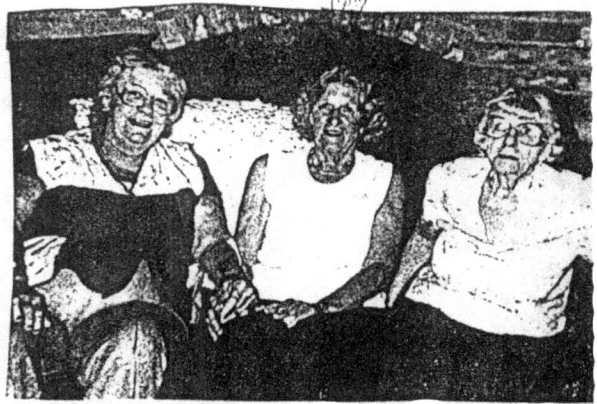

LUELLA *ANNA*LAURA
PAT   NANCY

WOODBURY FAMILY

CHARLIE, MAUDE, IVA, CECIL, HERMAN
LUELLA, NOLA

THE WOODBURY FAMILY   1953
HERMAN, ANNA, MAUDE, IVA, CECIL
LUELLA, NOLA, LAURA

EDDIE   NIBBS   JOHNNY
RAHM   HINDS   WOODBURY

LUELLA, NOLA, HERMAN, CHARLIE

WOODBURY FAMILY

NOLA WOODBURY

CHARLIE & NOLA
WOODBURY
1921

LAURA & NOLA WOODBURY

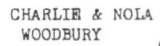

TOOTS, IN HER HEYDAY, GIVING RIDES TO CHILDREN
Picture taken in 1930 shows elephant with her trainer

ANNA WOODBURY'S BROTHER

SYLVESTER
&
MAUDE
CORNWILL

1953

FLORENCE   WILL
AUSTIN &   KRAPP
CORNWILL
KRAPP   ANNA WOODBURY'S
                     MOTHER

HERMAN ROY WOODBURY

HERMAN, THE FIRST CHILD OF JOHN & ANNA WOODBURY WAS BORN ON APR. 23, 1892, IN LENNAWEE CO., MI. HE MARRIED F. EMMA , THEY HAD THREE CHILDREN. SHE DIED IN THE LATE 1920'S HE THEN MARRIED RUTH , AND SHE RAISED HIS CHILDREN AS HER OWN. HERMAN PASSED AWAY IN FEB. OF 1975. RUTH PASSED AWAY IN FEB. 1984. THEY LIVED IN MERRITT, SISLAND, FLA.

JOHN WOODBURY, MARRIED CORRINE. THEY HAD SIX CHILDREN . THEY LIVE IN MERRITT ISLAND FLA.

    JACK,   HE LIVES IN CALIFORNIA
    JERRY, HE PASSED AWAY AS A CHILD IN SEPT. 1948
    BILL,
    LU ANN, MARRIED RALPH VASQUEZ, LIVES IN MERRITT, ISLAND, FLA.
    RODNEY,   LIVES IN CHARLOTT, N.C.
    JIM LIVES IN MERRITT ISLAND , FLA.

  HERMAN WOODBURY JR. HE MARRIED WILMA DINNEE. HERMAN DIED AT AGE 22, IN MAR, 1940. THEY HAD ONE CHILD.

 2/27/1939 DARLENE WOODBURY , MARRIED 1. PAT O'LEARY
               2. ARTHUR DUDLEY
    SHE HAS SIX CHILDREN & TWO STEP SONS.
  8/3/58 SHANNON O'LEARY MARRIED TO GUY BRIMMER (div.) , SHE HAS FOUR CHILDREN
     COLLEEN, JOLLEEN, SHAWN, & JOSH BRIMMER
  2/26/59 SHELLY O'LEARY, MARRIED TO RUSSELL BYRAM. THEY HAVE TWO CHILDREN.
     STACY & MICHELLE BYRAM
  7/28/60 KELLY O'LEARY, SHE HAS TWO CHILDREN.
     PATRICK & PENNY O'LEARY
  8/22/65 GREGORY O'LEARY, MARRIED TO ANGELIA. THEY HAVE 2 CHILDREN.
     JESSICA & GREGORY O'LEARY JR.
 TWIN 8/23/69 DAWN DUDLEY, SHE HAS TWO CHILDREN
     MISTY & BRANDON STREET
 TWIN 8/23/69 DIONE DUDLEY MARRIED TO JEFF ROLLINS. THEY HAVE THREE CHILDREN.
     ANTHONY , AMANDA ,& AARON ROLLINS.
    STEP-SONS
    ARTHUR DUDLEY JR. MARRIED TO FRANCIS, THEY HAVE THREE CHILDREN.
     SCOTT, JASON,& DANIEL DUDLEY
    LARRY DUDLEY, NOT MARRIED.

  OPAL WOODBURY, DIED AS A CHILD

HERMAN WOODBURY FAMILY

HERMAN & RUTH

JOHNY WOODBURY FAMILY 1953

JOHNNY* CORRINE
RON* LUANN* JIMMY

CORINE BILL RUTH JOHNNY HERMAN
WOODBURY

RUTH & HERMAN

Entered Into Eternal Rest
Tuesday, Feb. 4, 1975

HERMAN R. WOODBURY

Services for Herman Roy
Woodbury, 82, of 1767 Worley
Ave. Merritt Island, will be at
11 a.m. Saturday at Brevard
Funeral Home, Rockledge. He
died Tuesday at Cape Canav-
al Hospital, Cocoa Beach.
   He was a retired machinist

   Survivors include his wife,
Mrs. Ruth Woodbury; one son,
John Woodbury, Charlotte,
N.C.; three brothers, Cecil
Woodbury, Toledo, O., Charles
Woodbury, Pomona Park,
Fla., and Harry Woodbury,
Monroe, Mich.; five sisters,
Luella Hinds, Nola Roths, Iva
Gardner, Maudie Green, and
Laura Hinds, all of Toledo O.;
six grandchildren and 27
great-grandchildren.

HERMAN
WOODBURY JR.

Herman W. Woodbury, 22, of
Box 669, Route 8, West Toledo,
employe of the Toxilleather Corp.,
died in Toledo Hospital yesterday
following an illness of two weeks.
   A lifelong resident of Toledo, Mr.
Woodbury is survived by his wife,
Wilma; daughter, Darlene; par-
ents, Mr. and Mrs. Herman R.
Woodbury; brother, John, and
grandparents, Mr. and Mrs. John
Woodbury, all of Toledo.
   Services will be at 2:30 p. m.
Wednesday in the Boyer-Fellbach
Mortuary, Collingwood Memorial.
Burial will be in State Line Ceme-
tery.

HERMAN R. WOODBURY FAMILY

JOHNNY
WOODBURY

HERMAN
WOODBURY

LU ANN
WOODBURY

DARLENE WOODBURY

JOHNNY WOODBURY
&
BUD HINDS

DARLENE WOODBURY

JACK WOODBURY
&
RUTH WOODBURY

HERMAN WOODBURY FAMILY

HERMAN & RUTH
WOODBURY

LU ANN WOODBURY
VASQUEZ

BILL WOODBURY

RON JOHNNY JIMMY CORINE WOODBURY
& GRANDDAUGHTER

HERMAN WOODBURY FAMILY

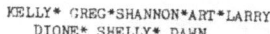

DUDLEY* O'LEARY FAMILY

GREG* SHANNON * ARTIE* LARRY

KELLY* SHELLY

DARLENE* DIONE* ART *DAWN

KELLY* GREG*SHANNON*ART*LARRY
DIONE* SHELLY* DAWN

DARLENE
&
ART

DUDLEY

DIONE & DAWN
DUDLEY

HERMAN WOODBURY FAMILY

ART & DARLENE
DUDLEY

SHELLY & RUSSELL
MICHELLE & STACY
BYRAM

FRANCIS & ART DUDLEY JR.
SCOTT* JASON* DANIEL

GREGORY & ANGELA O'LEARY
JESSICA* GREG JR.

HERMAN WOODBURY FAMILY

SHANNON* COLLEEN* JOLLEEN* SHAWN*JOSH BRIMMER

KELLY
PENNY& PATRICK
O'LEARY

LARRY
&
DAWN
&
MISTY
STREETS

JEFFERY& DIONE ROLLINS

MAUDE FLORENCE WOODBURY

MAUDE WAS BORN AUG.12, 1894 TO JOHN & ANNA WOODBURY IN LENNAWEE CO. .MI.
 SHE MARRIED 1. LOUIS SHANNAWAY. OF THIS MARRIAGE SHE HAD THREE CHILDREN.
AFTER LOIUS PASSED AWAY, SHE LATER MARRIED 2. BILL GREEN. MAUDE PASSED AWAY IN HER 80'S

         MARY SHANNAWAY, MARRIED ERNEST(PAT) WAGNER. THEY HAD THREE CHILDREN.
               CAROLYN, FRANCIS, &JESSIE WAGNER.

         LOUIS SHANNAWAY, MARRIED BARBRA STEWART, THEY HAD SIX CHILDREN.
          LOUIE & BARB BOTH PASSED AWAY IN FLORIDA.

     JESSIE SHANNAWAY, DIED IN WWII

MAUDE WOODBURY SHANNAWAY GREEN FAMILY

MAUDE

BILL GREEN

JESSIE SHANNAWAY

MAUDE* LOUIE* LOUIE* MARY SHANNAWAY

CAROLYN,
FRANCIS
JESSIE
WAGNER

MAUDE WOODBURY SHANNAWAY GREEN

MAUDE WOODB'RY
1958

LOUIE SHANNAWAY FAMILY   1963

MAUDE
WOODBURY
SHANNAWAY
GREEN
FAMILY

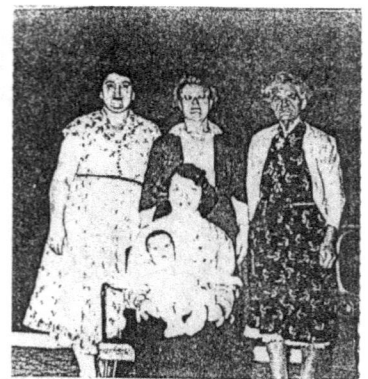

LOUIE& MARY
SHANNAWAY

MARY   MAUDE
WAGNER   GREEN   ANNA WOODBURY

            CAROLYN
               &
            DAUGHTER   5 GENERATIONS

LOUIE & BARB SHANNAWAY

HARRY FAY WOODBURY FAMILY

HARRY F. WOODBURY SON OF JOHN & ANNA WOODBURYWAS BORN IN LENNAWEE, CO. MI.
SEPT.12, 1897. HE MARRIED ALICE M. BOSENBARK ON SEPT. 2. 1920. OF THIS MARRIAGE
CAME THREE CHILDREN. HARRY PASSED AWAY DEC. 25,1981. ALICE IS STILL LIVING,
IN THE MONROE, MI. AREA.

RALPH WOODBURY, BORN OCT.8, 1928, MARRIED DONNA SYPE. THEY HADTWO CHILDREN,
HE PASSED AWAYADRIL, 16, 1986. HIS CHILDREN ARE, LORETTA KAY, AND RALPH JR.

HARRYF. WOODBURY JR. BORNFEB. 25, 197 , MARRIED MARY BURT. HE PASSED AWAY
APR. 1, 1981. THEY'HAD ONE CHILD. DANIEL W. WOODBURY.MARRIED TO ERLINA K.
VAN NORMAN. THEY HAVE THREE CHILDREN. DEBRA, CHRISTINA, MELISSA.

RAYMOND WOODBURY, BORN JULY 20,1933. HE MARRIED JOANN WOODBURY. HTEY HAVE THREE
CHILDREN.AND LIVE IN MONROE, MI. THERE CHILDREN ARE. THOMAS R. WOODBURY. MARRIED
TO ANNA CLARK. THEY HAVE THREE CHILDREN. LAURENA, RHIANNON, CARA.
SUSAN, AND THIMOTHY WOODBURY

HARRY F. WOODBURY

HARRY & CECIL
WOODBURY

Ex-bar owner H. Woodbury dies at 85

12-26-81

Harry F. Woodbury, 85, of 13781 LaPlaisance Rd., Bolles Harbor, former owner and operator of Harry's Place and of Woodbury's Bar, died about 9:15 p.m. Friday in Mercy Hospital Unit. He had been seriously ill for three weeks. (Picture, Page 2A)

Friends may call after 6 tonight in the Rupp Funeral Home, where Monroe Lodge 1503, Benevolent and Protective Order of Elks, will have memorial services at 7 p.m. Sunday and Carl F. Payson Post 60, American Legion, will have military services at 7:30 Sunday. Funeral services will be at 11 a.m. Monday in the funeral home with the Rev. Hugh C. White of St. Paul's United Methodist Church officiating. Burial will be in Roselawn Memorial Park Cemetery, LaSalle.

Mr. Woodbury had been employed by the Monroe Fire Department and by Willow Run Bomber Plant. In 1944 he bought a tavern on N. Monroe St. with his son, Harry Jr., which they called Harry's Place. They took over what became Woodbury's Bar on E. Front St. 18 months later and sold it when Harry Sr. retired in 1962.

Born Dec. 9, 1896 in Tecumseh, he was the son of John M. and Anna (Cornell) Woodbury. He married Alice M. Busenbark Sept. 2, 1920.

He served with the Army during World War I and with the Monroe Howitzer Company, Michigan National Guard, as a first lieutenant, during the 1920s.

He served as commander of Carl Payson Post 60, American Legion; was a member of Monroe Lodge 1503, BPOE, where he was named Elk of the Year in 1970; a member of Monroe County Voiture 1153, 40 et 8; Monroe Aerie 2254, Fraternal Order of Eagles; Robert A. Hutchinson Monroe Lodge 113, Fraternal Order of Police, and of the Monroe Senior Citizens.

Surviving are his wife; three sons, Ralph W., Raymond O., and Norman E., all of Monroe; a brother, Charles of Florida; two sisters, Mrs. Laura Hinds and Luella Hinds, both of Florida; six grandchildren, and eight great-grandchildren.

He was preceded in death by his son, Harry Jr.; two brothers, and two sisters.

CHARLES LEON WOODBURY

HE WAS BORN IN LENNAWEE CO. , MI. ON FEB. 29, 1899.. TO JOHN & ANNA WOODBURY.
HE MARRIED IVA DUTY . CHARLES DIED DEC.3, 1985. IVA PASSED AWAY IN APR. OF 1930.
        THEIR CHILDREN ARE: JUNE, CLARENCE,CHARLES. RALPH. HOWARD. GLADYS & CAROL
WOODBURY.   CHARLIE & IVA LIVED IN OHIO, NORTHERN MICHIGAN, & IN FLOIIDA.

CHARLES WOODBURY FAMILY

IVA & CHARLIE 1955

CHARLIE WOODBURY

CHARLES WOODBURY FAMILY

CHARLIE'S
FAMILY

Charles Woodbury

Charles I. Woodbury, 66, of Palatka, Fla., and formerly of Travis Drive, died December 3 in Putnam Memorial Hospital, Palatka. He had been employed at the Arklin Stamping Division, prior to moving to Florida 35 years ago. Surviving are his daughters, Mrs. June Hastings, Mrs. Gladys Paige, and Mrs. Carol Wolfe, sons Clarence, Ralph, and Charles and sisters, Mrs. Laura Hines, Mrs. Luella Hines and Mrs. Nola Bahm. Services were in the Masters Mortuary, Palatka.

IVA& CHARLIE
WOODBURY
&
KID'S

CAROL WOODBURY

CLARENCE& CAROLINE

CHARLIE WOODBURY'S
KID'S

LOYAL WOODBURY

BORN DEC. 24, 1901 IN LENNAWEE CO. ,MI. TO JOHN & ANNA WOODBURY. HE DIED APR. 23, 1903
AT 1½ YRS.

IVA IRENE MAY QUEEN WOODBURY

IVA WAS BORN IN LENNAWEE, CO.MI. , ON OCT.5, 1905, TO JOHN & ANNA WOODBURY.
SHE WAS MARRIED TO 1. RED HOUCK
                    2. ZENITH OSENBAUGH
                    3. ARTHUR SNYDER
                    4. JAMES EDINGTON

SHE WAS THE MOTHER OF 14 CHILDREN.
1/15/22 1. ALVIN L. WOODBURY , MARRIED TO MILLIE, THEY ARE THE PARENTS OF THREE BOYS
ALVIN & MILLIE LIVE IN APOPKA, FLA.
      DAVID A. WOODBURY MARRIED 1. KAY HANKENS
                        2. NORMA COFFELt
      DAVID HAS FOUR CHILDREN AND FIVE STEP-CHILDREN. DAVID LIVES IN TOLEDO,OH.
        DAVID ALVIN, ALAN RAY, CAROLYN,& DAVID ADAM WOODBURY, RAYMOND, RYAN, MICHAEL,
NANCY, & JILL OSENBAUGH.

        DARREL ANTHONY
        JOSEPH LEROY   BOTH ARE SINGLE AND LIVE AT HOME.

7/12/23 2. DORTHY HOUCK, MARRIED RICHARD BEATY. SHE PASSED AWAY IN NOV. 1984, RED, DIED IN DEC.1986
SHE HAD EIGHT CHILDREN. DELILAH, ROBERT, ROLAND , LARRY, CARL, PEGGY, TERRY, &RICHARD
BEATY. LARRY, WAS KILLED IN MAR. 1968.

    3. ZENITH (BABE) OSENBAUGH MARRIED 1. DORTHY
                              2. VIVIAN (DINK)
    HE HAS SEVEN CHILDREN, AND LIVES IN TOLEDO,OH.

    LINDA, ANNA, MARY, SHARON. JOHN. HOWARD, & DORTHY JEAN OSENBAUGH

    4. MILTON OSENBAUGH IS MARRIED TO MARY, HE HAS FIVE CHILDREN AND LIVES IN NEW YORK
        SHELIA, DEBBIE KATHY, JANET, JACKIE OSENBAUGH.

    5. ANNABELLE OSENBAUGH, KNAPP, LIVES IN LAKE CITY, MI.
              JOHN

    6. RUTH OSENBAUGH , MARRIED HARRY ROGERS THEY HAVE FOUR CHILDREN AND LIVE IN ALPENA, MI.
        GARY, VICKY, DONNA,&MICHAEL ROGERS

    7. CECIL OSENBAUGH , MARRIED JUDITH PRATT THEY LIVE IN CHARLOTTE. MI. AND HAVE FIVE
    CHILDREN AND NINE GRANDCHILDREN
            JUDY ELAINE, MARRIED CRAIG RAPPERT. THEY HAVE THREE CHILDREN. KAMRAN, CHANLER,
        MASON RAPPERT.

        ROBERT WAYNE, MARRIED TO ROBIN, THEY HAVE FOUR CHILDREN. WAYNE JEREMY. &LALENA
        OSENBAUGH. JENNIFER & WILLIAM HILDABRANT.

        FRANK SHERMAN, NOT MARRIED

        HARRY, MARRIED TO ANN, THEY HAVE TWO CHILDREN. ASHLEY NICOLE,& HARRY JR.
        OSENBAUGH

        CECIL JR. NOT MARRIED

    8. JOYCE OSENBAUGH , MARRIED 1. PETE STARKEY
                      2. DON SWIGEGOOD

IVA IRENE MAY QUEEN WOODBURY

JOYCE HAS SIX CHILDREN AND LIVES IN LIMA, OH.

JOANN& TERRY STARKEY, KAREN & SHAWN SWICEGOOD. TANYA & TODD ALLEN SERGENT.

7/10/35 9. BONNIE OSENBAUGH , MARRIED JAMES BROWN.. HE PASSED AWAY IN FEB. 1989.
THEY HAVE FOUR CHILDREN. BONNIE LIVES IN TOLEDO, OH.
1.NADAJABROWN, MARRIED TO CHARLES BONDY. NO CHILDREN
2. BONITA BROWN, MARRIED DANIEL WELSH, THEY HAVE TWO CHILDREN.
DARLEEN & DANETTE WELSH.
3. LORI BROWN MARRIED 1.KENNETH MASON
2.RAY OSENBAUGH
SHE HAS THREE CHILDREN, KENNETH JR. , PENNY. &JAMES MASON.
4.GENNA BROWN, MARRIED TO STEVEN GOMER. THEY HAVE FOUR CHILDREN.
CARRIE. MICHELLE, DAWN &PHILLIP GOMER.

1/16/37 10. BEVERLY OSENBAUGH , MARRIED TO HERBERT SLATER. HERB PASSED AWAY IN FEB. 1981.
THEY HAVE ONE SON. BEVERLY LIVES ON ALPENA , MI.
CHARLES E, SLATER, MARRIED TO SHIRLEY MAE, SYLVESTER. HE
HAS NO CHILDREN. THEY LIVE IN ALPENA , MI.

11. MARLENE OSENBAUGH, CROWDER HAS SIX CHILDREN. .LUANN, CHARLES, KENNETH KNAPP
BOBBY, SARAH, & CHERYL CROWDER.

12. SHARON OSENBAUGH.

13 ARTHUR JOHN SNYDER MARRIED VIRGINIA. THEY LIVE INWACHULA, FLA.
HE HAS DAUGHTERS JOYCE &JUDY, SONS JOHN JR. & DARREN. AND A STEP-DAUGHTER
AMY.

14. SHERMAN OSENBAUGH , DIED AT AGE 2, DEC.5, 1939

IVA WOODBURY HOUCK, OSENBAUGH, SNYDER, EDINGTON FAMILY

Iva Edington

Mrs. Iva I. Edington, 74, of 1405 Page St., died Monday in Eastview Nursing Home, where she had been a patient the last four months. She was the widow of James Edington. Surviving are her sons, Zenith, Melton, and Cecil Osenbaugh, Alvin Woodbury, and Arthur J. Snyder, and daughters, Mrs. Dorothy Beaty, Mrs. Annabelle Knapp, Mrs. Ruth Rogers, Mrs. Joyce Sergent, Bonnie Osenbaugh, Mrs. Beverly Slater, Mrs. Marlene Crowder, and Mrs. Sharon Reed. Services will be at 1 p.m. Thursday in the H.H. Birkenkamp Mortuary, Trilby, where the body will be after 7 tonight.

Zenith Osenbaugh

Zenith S. Osenbaugh, 59, of 5840 Clover Lane, died yesterday in Toledo Hospital.

Born in Putnam County, Mr. Osenbaugh lived in Toledo 40 years. He was employed 12 years at Cherry Auto Parts, retiring in 1983.

Surviving are his wife, Bernice E.; daughters, Mrs. Annabelle Knapp, of Lake City, Mich.; Mrs. Marlene Crowder, of Cocoa Beach, Fla.; Mrs. Bonnie Brown, Mrs. Beverly Slater, Mrs. Joyce Swicegood, and Rosemary Osenbaugh, all of Toledo; Mrs. Sharon Stager, of Santa Monica, Calif., and Mrs. Ruth Rogers, of Lachine, Mich.; sons, Thomas and Zenith C., of Toledo; Milton, of Montgomery, Ala., and Cecil, of Charlotte, Mich.; stepsons, Dale and Richard Nofzinger, of Adrian, Mich.; Donald Nofzinger, of Lansing, Mich.; Alvin Woodbury, of Toledo; stepdaughters, Mrs. Sharon Hanning, of Adrian; Mrs. Dorothy Batey, of Toledo; brothers, Glen, of Lambertville, Mich.; Vern, of Toledo; sister, Mrs. Verda Helwig, of Ruskin, Fla.; half brothers, Gail Lindhorst, of Toledo; Dale Lindhorst, of East Harbor; half sisters, Mrs. Wilma Hahn, of Lambertville; Mrs. Julia Markham, of Toledo; 29 grandchildren, 13 stepgrandchildren, and 6 greatgrandchildren.

Services will be Wednesday at 3 p.m. in the H. H. Birkenkamp Mortuary, Trilby, with burial in Toledo Memorial Park.

BEVERLY* RUTH* JOYCE* BONNIE
OSENBAUGH

ANNABELE

IVA WOODBURY HOUCK OSENBAUGH SNYDER EDINGTON

IVA   1958

CHARLIE & BEVERLY
SLATER   1973

IVA WOODBURY HOUCK*OSENBAUGH * SNYDER' EDINGTON

DAVID*   MILLIE * ALVIN* WOODBURY

IVA WOODBURY, HOUCK, OSENBAUGH, SNYDER EDINGTON FAMILY

DELILAH
BEATY
LEBOWSKY

CARL
BEATY

DORTHY
HOUCK
BEATY

PEGGY
BEATY

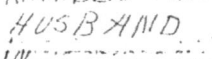

ANNABELE AND
HUSBAND
IN

ANNABELE

SCHOOL DAYS 1953-54
EAU GALLIE

JOHN SNYDER

IVA WOODBURY, HOUCK , OSENBAUGH, SNYDER, EDINGTON FAMILY

DINK & BABE

SHARON OSENBAUGH

ANNA
OSENBAUGH

JOHN OSENBAUGH

HOWARD
OSENBAUGH

LINDA
OSENBAUGH

CECIL WOODBURY

CECIL WAS BORN TO JOHN AND ANNA WOODBURY ON MAR. 4 , 1907. ON OCT.13, 1933 HE MARRIED IDABELLE LONG. CECIL WORKED MANY YEARS FOR THE WYLLYS-OVERLAND JEEP CO. CECIL PASSED AWAY IN JUNE OF 1976 OF CANCER. IDABELLE PASSED AWAY IN FEB. 1978.
THEY HAD TWO CHILDREN,AND SIX GRANDCHILDREN.   THEY LIVE IN TOLEDO. OH.

7/13/34   1. EDITH WOODBURY MARRIED DALE MUSSER OF THIS MARRIAGE THERE ARE FOUR CHILDREN.

  1/15/52   DALE A. MUSSER, MARRIED TO GERRI. THEY HAVE TWO SONS. JAMES& BRIAN MUSSER. THEY LIVE IN TOLEDO, OH

  5/9/53   ROBERT E, MUSSER , MARRIED TO TERESA. THEY HAVE THREE CHILDREN, JULIE, LAURA, JENIFFER MUSSER. THEY LIVE IN MONCLOVA. OH.

TWIN   7/9/57   LARRY D. MUSSER , MARRIED 1. DONNA STUCKY
                                      2. RENEA MEYERS
            LARRY HAS FIVE CHILDREN, HE LIVES IN SYLVANIA, OH.
  JEFFERY, MELISSA, HEATHER, LARRY M.II, &BRANDY MUSSER

TWIN   7/9/57   GARY D. MUSSER , MARRIED 1. PANELLA WILLIAMS
                                      2. DONNA PLAIR
      GARY HAS THREE CHILDREN & THREE STEP CHILDREN.
        GARY, MICHEAL, &NAISSA MUSSER.
      GARY LIVES IN S. MIDDLEBURG , FLA.

2. CECIL WOODBURY JR. MARRIED TO DELORES . OF THIS MARRIAGE THERE ARE TWO CHILDREN
      CECIL LIVES IN TOLEDO, OH.

CECIL WOODBURY FAMILY

CECIL* EDITH* IDABELLE & DALE JR.

EDITH

CECIL JR.

CECIL & IDABELLE

CECIL, IDABELLE, EDITH
WOODBURY

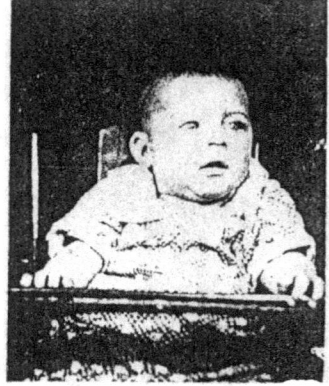

EDITH
WOODBURY
1934

CECIL JR., EDITH
WOODBURY

Cecil Woodbury, Sr.

Jeep Worker 43 Years, Helped
Operate Northgate Service Center

Cecil A. Woodbury, Sr., 68, of 5237
Belpre Dr., died Saturday in his home.

He worked 43 years for the Kaiser Jeep
Corp., retiring as a machinist in the metallurgy laboratory in 1969. In retirement he
helped his son, Cecil A., Jr., operate
Northgate Service Center, a business machine service firm.

He was a past patron of Fort Industry
Chapter, Order of Eastern Star; member
of Fort Industry Lodge, F&AM; past board
member of Fort Industry Rainbow Girls,
and member of Zenobia Shrine and O-Ton-
Ta-La Grotto.

Also surviving are his wife, Idabelle;
daughter, Mrs. Edith Musser; brothers,
Harry and Charles, and sisters, Mrs.
Maude Green, Mrs. Iva Ellington, Mrs.
Luella Hinds, Mrs. Laura Hinds, and Mrs.
Nola Carr.

Services will be at 11 a.m. Tuesday in
the Boyer-Van Wormer Mortuary, Secor
Road, where Masonic services will be at 8
p.m. Monday.

Idabelle Woodbury

Retired Beauty Operator Was Active
In Toledo, Area Eastern Star Circles

Mrs. Idabelle Woodbury, 80, of 5237 Belpre
Dr., a retired beauty operator and for many
years active in Toledo and area Order of
Eastern Star circles, died Tuesday in
Hawthorne, Calif., where she had been
visiting her sister, Grace Long.

Mrs. Woodbury had operated several local
beauty shops and had been an instructor at
the Toledo Academy of Beauty Culture 17
years, retiring in 1970. During her years of
activity in the OES, Mrs. Woodbury held
many offices. Among these were past matron of Fort Industry chapter; past Mighty
Choose of O-Ton-Ta-La-Caldron; and past
president, mother adviser, and board member of Fort Industry Business Rainbow
Girls. She also held various offices in
Dendarah Court, Ladies Oriental Shrine of
North America. She was the widow of Cecil
Woodbury, Sr., who died in July of 1976.

Also surviving are her son, Cecil, Jr.;
daughter, Mrs. Edith Musser; brothers,
William and Owen Long, and sisters, Mrs.
Jessie Brieau, and Mrs. Ethyl Flick.

Services will be Saturday at 1 p.m. in the
Boyer-Van Wormer-Scott Mortuary, Secor
Road. Eastern Star services will be Friday
at 7:30 p.m. in the mortuary.

CECIL WOODBURY FAMILY

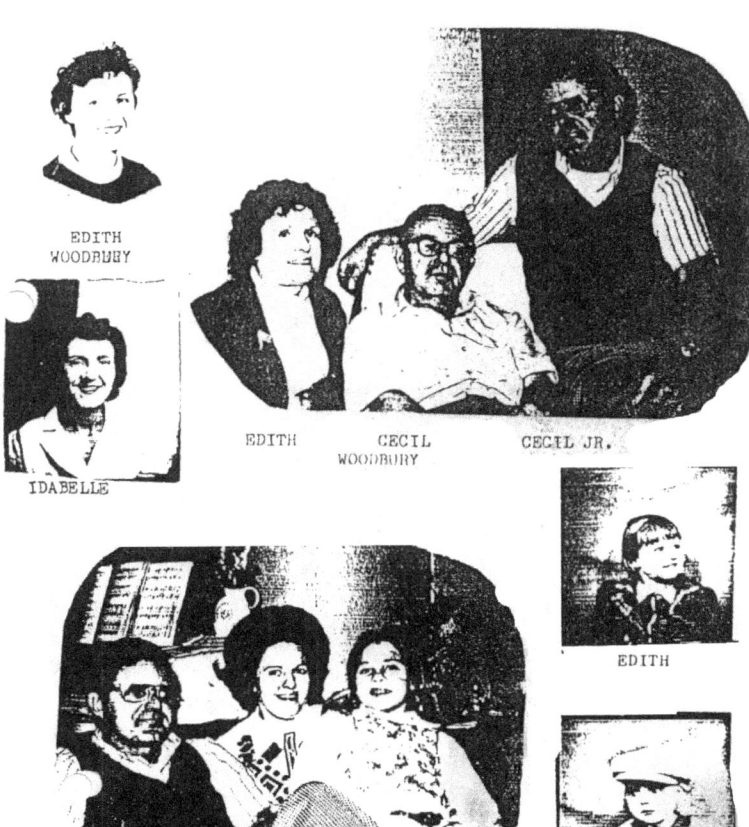

EDITH
WOODBURY

IDABELLE

EDITH   CECIL
          WOODBURY

CECIL JR.

EDITH

CECIL JR.   DELORES   SHERIE

CECIL JR.

LUELLA BELL WOODBURY(HINDS)

LUELLA WAS BORN IN MONROE, MI. ON JUNE 18, 1910 TO JOHN AND ANNA WOODBURY.   SHE MARRIED
ELI B. HINDS(BUD). THEY HAD ONE CHILD. BUD PASSED AWAY IN NOV. OF 1961. LUELLA LIVES WITH
HER DAUGHTER IN SYLVANIA, OH.

9/28/ 39   CHARMAYNE HINDS MARRIED DONALD GOCHENOUR, OF THIS MARRIAGE THERE ARE FOUR
CHILDREN
6/11/61   1. JENNIFER ANN GOCHENOUR. MARRIED TO DOUGLAS FINCH IN NOV. 1984, THEY HAVE
A DAUGHTER KALEIGH ASHTON FINCH

9/3/62   2. JEFFREY ALLEN GOCHENOUR   NOT MARRIED, LIVES AT HOME

TWINS   3. JON DONALD GOCHENOUR
                                    BOTH ARE UNMARRIED AND LIVING AT HOME
10/19/68   4. JAY ROBERT GOCHENOUR

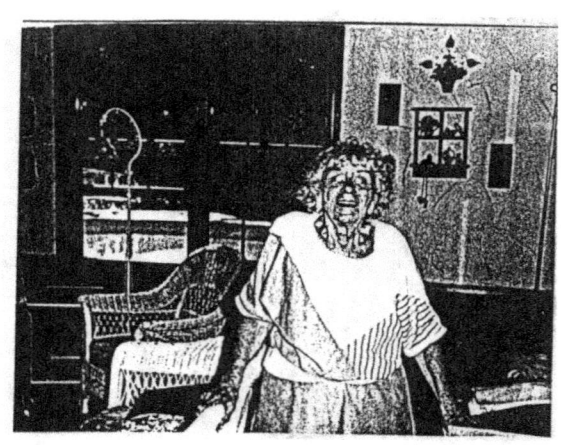

LUELLA WOODBURY HINDS FAMILY

BUD

LUELLA
WOODBURY

ELROY
BUD
HINDS

MAUDE* LUELLA *IVA
WOODBURY

LUELLA
NANCY & PATTY
HINDS

BUD HINDS

LUELLA WOODBURY HINDS FAMILY

LUELLA WOODBURY

LUELLA

LUELLA & ANNA WOODBURY

LUELLA & BUD HINDS

CHARMAYNE HINDS

LUELLA WOODBURY HINDS FAMILY

LUELLA   BUD & CHARMAYNE HINDS

PAT O'LEARY

DON & CHARMAYNE'S
WEDDING

DON & CHARMAYNE GOCHENOUR

LUELLA
CHARMAYNE
&
BUD
HINDS

LUELLA
&
LAUHA
HINDS

LUELLA WOODBURY HINDS FAMILY

Commissioners Refuse Demands Made by Unemployed Committee

Report Jobless Group May Again Attempt To Pitch Camp in Courthouse Park

SEVERAL demands, made by a committee of the Lucas County Council of Unemployed, including the removal of Sheriff Gilson D. Light, were refused by the county commissioners late yesterday.

The unemployed committee, which included Kenneth Eggert, Louie Borer, Louella Woodbury and W. Hastings, also demanded that the commissioners take immediate action to relieve conditions in Washington township. George W. Winters, president of the board, said the commissioners are powerless and advised the committee to confer with the township trustees. He added that should the trustees fail to act, the committee should take the matter up with the county prosecutor.

The committee also requested the commissioners to pay for damage done to the unemployed property when the sheriff made them remove their tents from the courthouse lawn Saturday. This request also was refused by the commissioners.

It was reported that because of the commissioners' refusal of the request the unemployed again may att to pitch camp on the cou. se lawn, from which they were evicted last Saturday.

It was considered doubtful, however, that the jobless would succeed in pitching camp on the lawn, since the commissioners have issued orders to the sheriff's office to prohibit them from even standing on the grass. They have been ordered to confine their mass meetings to the vicinity of McKinley's monument on the wide cement walk.

Mr. Winters informed the committee that the commissioners are doing everything in their power to put into effect legislation they have passed, calling for a bond issue that would make available at once $50,000 for poor relief in Washington township.

LUELLA

JENNY
JEFF
JON& JAY
GOCHENOUR

COTTAGES AT VINEYARD LAKE

CHARMAYNE HINDS

CHARMAYNE
HINDS

DON*JENNIFER
CHARMAYNE*JEFFREY
JON*JAY
GOCHENOUR

LUELLA WOODBURY HINDS FAMILY

JEFF & LUELLA

DON & CHARMAYNE GOCHENOUR

JENNIFER
GOCHENOUR

CHARMAYNE

KALEIGH FINCH

CHARMAYNE
HINDS

CHARMAYNE

ANNIBELE WOODBURY

DAUGHTER OF JOHN AND ANNA WOODBURY, SHE WAS BORN ABOUT 1913(SHE DIED ABOUT FOUR YEARS LATET OF BLOOD POISONING FROM A BLISTER ON HER HEEL.

LAURA LOUISE WOODBURY (HINDS)

LAURA WAS BORN ON AUG. 19, 1916, TO JOHN AND ANNA WOODBURY. ON JULY 22, 1933 IN MONROE , M.
SHE MARRIED HARTLEY W. HINDS. OF THIS MARRIAGE CAME 11 CHILDREN, AND A SET OF TWINS WHO DIEI
AT BIRTH. LAURA PASSED AWAY IN AUG.OF 1989, IN NAPLES, FLA. NIBBS DIED IN MAY OF 1985 IN
NAPLES,

       PAT   MARRIED 1.PAUL MORRIS   (div.)
       LOCKWOOD   2. ROBERT MC KINNEY   "
                         3. CARL LOCKWOOD   "   SHE LIVES IN NAPLES, FLA.

          DEBRA MORRIS, PAUL MORRIS, PAMELA MORRIS, RICKMC KINNEY, ROBERT(PEANUT) MC KINNEY
          MARK MC KINNEY.

       NANCY
       COATS   MARRIED FREEMAN COATS   NANCY PASSED AWAY OF CANCER IN 1989

          MARY,KAREN,JAMES, FREEMAN JR., BUG'S COATS

724/1938JERRY
     HINDS   MARRIED SHIRLEY JEAN ECKHART THEY LIVE IN NAPLES, FLA

         JERRY HINDS JR.

         SHERRY HINDS   SHE MARRIED JOE IMBIMBO(div.)
                   SHE HAS THREE CHILDREN
                   TWINS, CHARLENE&DARLENE , AND BOBBY HINDS

8/ 23/   RICHARD HINDS MARRIED TO SHELBY PIERCE, THE HAVE TWO CHILDREN
                     RICHARD HINDS JR.
                     PHYLLIS "

              RICHARD DRIVES TRUCK, AND LIVES ON PEIDMONT, ALA.

716/   SUE HINDS MARRIED 1. DALE LYONS
                        2. JIM KERTZ

              SHE HAS FOUR CHILDREN AND SIX GRAND CHILDREN. AND LIVES IN NAPLES, FLA.

          DONNIE, RANDY, & WANDA LYONS , & JAMIE KERTZ

       ANNA MARIE HINDS, DIED IN CHILDHOOD

5/20/ 1944 TOM HINDS   MARRIED 1. GRACE ECKHART
                                 2. BONNIE
                                 3. ANN
                                 4. DONNA
          TOM HAS 15 CHILDREN.
            LORETTA, LARRY. DEBBIE HINDS, & MARIE, TOMMY, MARGIE, MARY HINDS& TOMMY,
          TWINS TERRI& KERRILYNN. DIANA MAE, JOEY HINDS & CYNTHIA, DONALD ,RICHARD MANNON

LAURA WOODBURY HINDS FAMILY

JIM HINDS MARRIED TO PATTY HALL, THEY LIVE IN NAPLES , FLA. THEY HAVE THREE CHILDREN AND ONE GRAND CHILD.

JIM JR. EVELYN, ANNIE HINDS

KATHY HINDS MARRIED 1. JAKE CULBREATH
                      2. RANDY BIBBEE

SHE HAS FOUR CHILDREN AND SEVEN GRAND-CHILDREN

TIM, LAURA, SAM, MERT CULBREATH

KEITH HINDS MARRIED TO LUCINDA, HE LIVES IN NAPELS , FLA. AND THEY HAVE NO CHILDREN.

BILL HINDS MARRIED TO GEORGETTE, THEY LIVE IN FT. LAUDERDALE, FLA THEY HAVE TWO CHILDREN.
                 BILL HINDSJR. & CHRISTINE HINDS

July 20 7983

Open House In Naples, Fla., Planned For Hartley Hindses

Mr. and Mrs. Hartley Hinds, of Naples, Fla., and formerly of Yarmouth Avenue, will observe their 50th wedding anniversary from noon to 6 p.m. Saturday with an open house given by their children in Naples.

They were married July 22, 1933 in Monroe, Mich. Mrs. Hinds is the former Laura Woodbury.

Mr. Hinds is a retired truck driver.

The couple have sons, Jerry, Richard, Tom, Jim, Keith, and Bill, and daughters, Mrs. Patsy Lockwood, Mrs. Nancy Coats, Mrs. Sandra Kertz, and Mrs. Kathy Bibbee. They also have 41 grandchildren and 31 great-grandchildren.

Mr. and Mrs. Hinds

LAURA WOODBURY HINDS FAMILY

LAURA & NIBBS HINDS
50th. ANNINERSARY
1983

HINDS FAMILY

JIM* KEITH*TOM* NANCY* KATHY*RICHARD
SUE*PAT*NIBBS* LAURA*JERRY

UDY NAHM   KATHY

SUE   WANDA

LAURA

LAURA* KATHY* SUE HINDS

LAURA& NIBBS HINDS

LAURA HINDS

LAURA WOODBURY HINDS FAMILY

KATHY
HINDS

LAURA * NANCY & KIDS IN FLA.

JERRY HINDS

LAURA & NIBBS 50th.ANNIVERSARY
WITH GRAND KIDS

PATTY
HINDS

LAURA WOODBURY HINDS FAMILY

PAT& LAURA HINDS

PAM* PAUL* DEBBY MORRIS BILL &KEITH HINDS
PEANUT & RICK MC KINNEY

HINDS FAMILY

JIM*
TOM* SUE* KATHY DIANNA * LAURA & FRED
RAHN

SHELBY
RICHARD JR. WANDA LYON

THE MC KINNEY FAMILY

R T U & DEBBY MORRIS

DEBBY

THE HINDS FAMILY

PATTY HINDS

PAT HINDS

LAURA WOODBURY HINDS FAMILY

NANCY HINDS

NANCY

NANCY

PATTY & NANCY
HINDS

LAURA WOODBURY HINDS FAMILY
JERRY & JERRY JR.

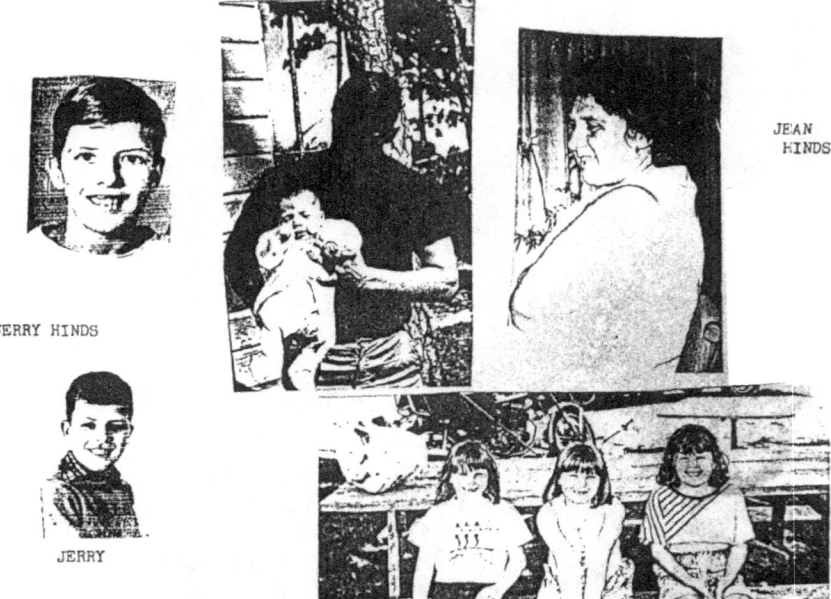

JERRY HINDS

JERRY

JEAN
HINDS

DARLENE * CHARLENE & BOBBY HINDS

JEAN & JERRY HINDS
1991

LAURA WOODBURY HINDS FAMILY

RICHARD HINDS

RICHARD JR. & PHYLLIS HINDS

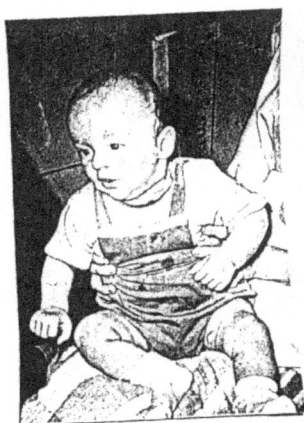

RICHARD JR.

RICHARD SHELBY & RICHARD JR.
HINDS

LAURA WOODBURY HINDS FAMILY

SUE

JIM , SUE & JAMIE KERTZ

SUE DALE
WANDA* RANDY* DONNIE
LYONS

JUDY   * SUE   * NANCY   LAURA
RAHM   KATHY   DEBBY * KEITH

HINDS

THE HINDS FAMILY 1953

LAURA WOODBURY HINDS FAMILY

TOM HINDS

RICHARD * CYNTHIA * DONALD

TOM & DONNA HINDS

NOLA MAE WOODBURY (RAHM)

NOLA WAS BORN TO JOHN & ANNA WOODBURY ON AUG. 23, 1919. ON MAY 9,1934 SHE MARRIED
ARD J. RAHM. OF THIS MARRIAGE CAME THREE CHILDREN. NOLA PASSED AWAY. APR. 17, 1990.
O. KIDNEY DISEASE. EDWARD PASSED AWAY FEB. 22, 1972, OF MUSCULAR DYSTROPHY. THEY OWNED
MULBERRY T.V. IN TOLEDO, OH. THEY RETIRED TO FT. MYERS, FLA. IN 1965, AND LIVED THERE
UNTIL EDDIES DEATH.

2/2/1938
1. EDWARD J. RAHM II   MARRIED PATRICA   THEY HAD TWO CHILDREN , AND ARE NOW DIVORCED.
    8/30/1969 LUANN RAHM   MARRIED 1. TIM GIBSON(div.)
                                     2. GARY COLE
                                            AMANDA& JESSICA GIBSON
                                            MARISSA COLE

        11/7/1979   EDWARD RAHM IV

        HE LIVES IN TOLEDO, OH.

    4/14/1941
2. JUDY ANN RAHM   MARRIED MURIEL ROGERS   THEYHAD FOUR GIRLS, TWO PASSED AWAY AT BIRTH.
JUDY PASSED AWAY IN JUNE OF 1988, AFTERBEEING PARALYZED IN 1985 FROM TRANSVERSEMALITES.
MURIEL PASSED AWAY IN 1989.

10/10/1962   CHRISTINA ROGERS, MARRIED JEFF LEICHTY THEY HAVE SEVEN CHILDREN
             STEVEN. & MICHAEL ROGERS, CHRISTOPHER, MICHELLE, ROBBIE, AND TWINS JOSHUA&
             JACOB LEICHTY.

 9/1967   CHERYL ROGERS. SHE IS NOT MARRIED

    THEY LIVE IN CAPE CORAL , FLA.

7/10/1945
3. DIANNA MAE RAHM MARRIED 1. JERRY MC CAUSLIN(DIV.)
                            2. ALLEN J. PARKER

    SHE HAS ONE CHILD.

            ALAN J. PARKER BORN NOV. 21, 1983

    THEY LIVE IN PERRYSBURG, OH.

NOLA WOODBURY RAHM

NOLA 1959

EDDIE RAHM
1953

NOLA RAHM
1956

NOLA WOODBURY RAHM FAMILY

NOLA & EDDIE RAHM   1956

EDWARD RAHM & NOLA WOODBURY
WEDDING PICTURE

•NOLA RAHM

Nola Rahm, 70, died Tuesday. April 17, 1990, in Wood ~unty Nursing Home, Bowl-; Green.

Mrs. Rahm was born in Monroe, Michigan, to John and Anna (Cornwill) Woodbury. She married Edward J. Rahm on May 9, 1934, in Monroe, Michigan. After living in Sylvania they moved to Toledo where they opened Mulberry TV, retiring to Florida in 1966. He preceded her in death in 1972.

She moved to McAuley Court In 1982.

She was a member of the Rossford Eagles Auxiliary.

Surviving are a son, Edward, Jr., Toledo; daughter, Mrs. Diane Parker, Perrysburg; sister, Luella Hinds; five grandchildren and nine great-grandchildren.

Services were held April 20 in H.H. Birkenkamp Funeral Home, Toledo. Burial was at Toledo Memorial Park, Sylvania.

MARRIAGE LICENSE
MAY. 9, 1934

Seek License in Monroe
Edward J. Rahm, 21, and Nola M. Woodbury, 17, both of Toledo, applied for a marriage license Wednesday in Monroe, Mich

EDWARD RAHM
Edward J. Rahm Sr., 59, of 1155 Cherokee, Lehigh Acres, died Sunday. He moved to Lee County in 1966.
Survivors include his widow, Mrs. Nola Rahm, of Lehigh Acres; a son, Edward J. Rahm Jr., of Toledo, Ohio; daughters, Mrs. Judy Rogers, Mrs. Dianna McCauslin of Fort Myers and three grandchildren.
The body will be sent today to H. H. Birkenkamp Funeral Home, at Telby, Toledo, Ohio, for service and burial. Leo W. Engelhardt Funeral Home is in charge of local arrangements. Friends may call at the funeral home until ... today.

NOLA WOODBURY RAHM FAMILY

EDDIE& SONNY RAHM
JUDY& DIANNA

DIANNA * SONNY* JUDY RAHM

SONNY& NOLA RAHM

MARLENE   & SONNY   NOLA

1989

Television Repair Shop Helped Man To Successfully Overcome Disability

Service Calls Made By Wife When Disease Progressed

By EDWIN BOWERS
Blade Staff Writer

The television repair shop on Mulberry Street is more than just another family-owned business. It is the product of two persons' successful efforts to overcome a serious handicap.

The shop, now a thriving business, was started almost 20 years ago in Sylvania in the home of Mr. and Mrs. Edward Rahm when Mr. Rahm became so disabled by multiple sclerosis that he had to quit his job in a paint and metal shop.

Business was slow at first even though Mr. Rahm's hobby was electronics and he had repaired and assembled many radios in his spare time.

"Many a time we would use the grocery money for a repair job, then wait for the customer to come in pay for the job before we got a square meal again," Mrs. Rahm said. She added that they sold the family car to stock the shop when they first started.

Disease Progressed

When Mr. Rahm's disease progressed to the point that he could no longer make service calls, Mrs. Rahm took over these chores.

"When I made my first service call, I was pretty worried. But it turned out to be a pleasant surprise. The people thought it was interesting to have a woman work on their set," Mrs. Rahm said.

Business improved greatly for the Rahms in the 1950's when television became popular.

Mr. Rahm said that when the first sets were sold a few years after World War II, he had already studied television circuits to prepare himself for any repair jobs that might come his way. He and his wife used to sit up at night and wind coils to build their own set.

The shop grew so much in the next 10 years that the Rahms decided to move into Toledo, and in 1957 they moved to Mulberry Street.

Left Sylvania

When they left Sylvania, they carried a stock of 125 tubes. Today the shop stocks more than 3,000 and the number constantly increases. Mr. Rahm said. Much of the new stock is to service color television which, he said, has caused a real boom for the television repairman.

A particularly successful economic venture has been the conversion of small transistor radios from FM to police bands.

—Blade Photo

LEARNING A TRADE AT HOME CAN BE FUN
Mr. and Mrs. Rahm discuss a repair job with their son

Mr. Rahm bought the radios then changed the circuits to pick up the higher police frequency. These radios, he said, have become very popular.

Looking back over the years in which his business became a success, Mr. Rahm feels the best part about it was the people he met and friends he made. He is particularly happy that his son, Edward, Jr., now has taken over the business.

Mrs. Rahm said she felt good getting the three children reared and educated. With this over she was ready to retire.

So — last week the Rahms retired and moved to Fort Myers, Fla., where they will take up permanent residence.

NOLA WOODBURY RAHM FAMILY

JUDY RAHM

KELLY
O'LEARY

MURIEL
&
CHRISTINA
ROGERS

SHELLY
O'LEARY

SONNY
RAHM

DIANNA RAHM

Lot of Love
Sonny
'55

NOLA WOODBURY RAHM FAMILY

SONNY & PATTY & LUANN RAHM

EDDIE
RAHM
IV

LUANN & EDDIE RAHM IV

AMANDA & JESSICA GIBSON

MARISSA COLE

Judy Rogers

Mrs. Judy R. Rogers, 47, of Mott Avenue, died Tuesday in Parkview Hospital. She was a seasonal worker at Hunt Wesson Foods for two years. Surviving are her husband, Mearl; daughters, Cheryl and Mrs. Christina Leichty; mother, Mrs. Nola Rahm; brother, Sonny Rahm, and sister, Mrs. Diana Parker. The body will be in the H.H. Birkenkamp Mortuary, Trilby, after 5 today. Graveside services will be at 10 a.m. tomorrow in Toledo Memorial Park.

CHERYL

JUDY

MURIEL

Muriel Rogers

Muriel H. Rogers, 64, of Fort Smith, Ark., and formerly of Toledo, died Thursday in Spark Hospital, Fort Smith. He was a metal finisher for the Jeep Corp., 31 years, retiring in 1985. He was the widower of Judy Rogers. Surviving are daughters, Mrs. Christina Leichty and Cheryl Rogers; brother, Earl Rogers, and five grandchildren. Graveside services will be at 2 p.m. Monday in the Toledo Memorial Cemetery. There will be no visitation. Arrangements are by the Edwards Mortuary, Fort Smith.

NOLA WOODBURY RAHM FAMILY

STEVEN
ROGERS

JEFF * MIKE* CHRISSY
JACOB & JOSH
CHRISTOPHER * MICHELLE * ROBBIE
LEICHTY

JUDY
RAHM
ROGERS

JUDY
JUDY ROGERS 1983

JUDY & MURIEL CHERYL * CHRISSY& JEFF
STEVE ROGERS   LEICHTY
     * MIKE   MICHELLE CHRISTOPHER

NOLA   WOODBURY   RAHM   FAMILY

JUDY &   DIANNA
RAHM

TOMMY HINDS

JUDY&CHARMAYNE &DIANNA

NOLA RAHM

ALAN PARKER

ALAN
PARKER

AL & DIANNA PARKER   NOLA RAHM

WOODBURY TWINS

    TWINS ARE VERY COMMON IN THE WOODBURY FAMILY. IN THE LAST THREE GENERATIONS, THERE HAVE BEEN SEVEN SETS BORN.
    HERMAN'S GRANDDAUGHTER, DARLENE DUDLEY, HAS TWIN GIRLS. DAWN & DIONE
    CHARLIE'S SON CHARLES, HAD TWIN GIRLS,? I BELIEVE.
    CECIL'S DAUGHTER EDITH, HAD SONS LARRY & GARY MUSSER
    LUELLA'S DAUGHTER CHARMAYNE, HAD TWIN SONS JAY & JON GOCHENOUR.
    LAURA HAD TWINS THAT DIED AT BIRTH, IN THE MID-FIFTIES. ALSO LAURA'S SON TOM HAS TWIN DAUGHTERS, TERIE LYNN & KERIE LYNN, AND HER SON JERRY HAS TWIN GRANDAUGHTERS CHARLENE & DARLENE HINDS.
    NOLA'S GRANDDAUGHTER CHRISTINA HAD TWINS, JOSHUA & JACOB LEICHTY.

    THESE ARE THE ONES WE COULD REMEMBER, IF YOU HAVE ANY INFORMATION ON ANY OTHERS PLEASE LET ME KNOW.

LARRY & GARY MUSSER
JULY 9. 1957
GRANDSONS OF CECIL WOODBURY

DARLENE & CHARLENE HINDS DEC. 30, 1984
GR-GRANDDAUGHTERS OF LAURA HINDS

Sylvanian named Mother of Year
~y Mother of Twins Club

Mrs. Charmayne Gochenour has been selected the Toledo Mother of the Year by members of the Mothers of Twins Club.

Mrs. Gochenour has been a member of the club since 1968 and has served on many committees in addi-

tion to being president in 1974-75.

She and her husband, Don, reside at 5261 Tavistock Drive, and have four children. A daughter is a freshman in college, one son is a high school senior

and the twins are 11 years old.

She is an active member, with her husband, of St. Joseph's Church. She also assists with various community activities in addition to keeping house and attending college part time.

GOCHENOUR TWINS

JAY & JON
OCT. 19, 1968
GRANDSONS OF LUELLA HINDS

Proud

John, left, and Jay Gochenour glance proudly at their mother, Mrs. Charmayne Gochenour, who was recently named Toledo Mother of the Year by the Toledo Mother of Twins Club.

JAY & JON

DAWN & DIONE DUDLEY

AUG 23, 1969   DUDLEY
TWINS

HERMAN
WOODBURY'S
GREAT GRAND
DAUGHTERS

DAWN & DIONE   1984

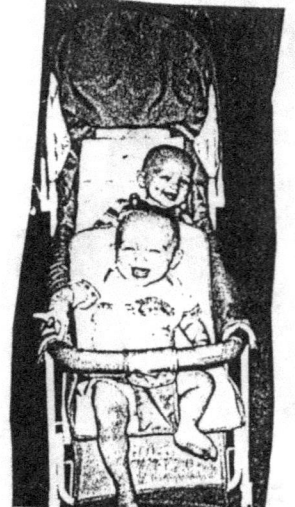

JOSHUA
&
JACOB
LEICHTY

GREAT
GRANDSONS OF
NOLA
WOODBURY
RAHM

DEC. 26, 19 89

OTHER WOODBURY REUNIONS
WERE YOU HERE?

OTHER WOODBURY REUNIONS
WERE YOU HERE?

Woodbury

Reunion

1994

WOODBURY
NEWS

AUGUST 28 1994   WOODBURY REUNION A CELEBRATION OF FAMILY

HERE IT IS!!! REUNION DAY AGAIN. THE THEME OF THIS YEARS REUNION IS
CELEBRATION OF FAMILY. SO TODAY WE HONOR THE MEMORY OF MAUDE WOODBURY,
SHE WAS BORN AUGUST 12, 100 YEARS AGO. MAUDE PASSED AWAY IN 1977,SHORTLY
BEFORE HER 83rd. BIRTHDAY.SO TODAY LET US ALL REMEMBER HER AND HER
FAMILY, AS WE CELEBRATE TODAY.
   FIRST I WISH TO WELCOME ALL OF YOU TO THE 1994 WOODBURY REUNION. IF THIS IS
THE FIRST TIME OR YOU HAVE BEEN HERE BEFORE, I HOPE YOU WILL ENJOY
YOURSELF, AND TAKE MANY GREAT MEMORIES HOME WITH YOU.
   WE WOULD LIKE TO WELCOME SOME NEW WOODBURY FAMILY MEMBERS . SELENA CAMPOSE,
SHE WAS MARRIED TO RICHARD SPRAGUE ON NOV. 24,1993 IN ORLANDO, FLA.. HE IS
THE   GRAND-SON OF LOUIE & BARB SHANNAWAY. ALSO WE WELCOME SOME NEW BIRTHS
IN THE FAMILY. DESTINY ANN MARIE SPRAGUE, BORN JUNE 6,1994. STEPHANIE LEIGH
CALHOUN, BORN OCT. 1,1993 GR-GR-GRAND CHILDREN OF MAUDE. NICHOLAS KEITH
PAYNE. BORN DEC. 23, 1993 HE IS THE GR-GRANDSON OF NANCY HINDS. PLEASE LET ME
KNOW OF ANY BIRTH, MARRIAGES,DEATHS, OR ANY FAMILY INFORMATION, FOR OUR
NEWS LETTERS.
   I WOULD LIKE TO SEND OUT THE GOOD WISHES OF ALL THE FAMILY TO BILL WOODBURY,
AND TO JOHN SPANGLER WHO HAVE BEEN ILL. AND TO RICHARD HINDS, JIMMY HINDS,
BABE & DINK OSENBAUGH, IT;S GOOD TO HEAR YOU ARE ALL GETTING BACK TO HEALTH.
   NOW FOR TODAY: WE HAVE THE HORSESHOE TOURNAMENT, IT IS OPEN TO BOTH MEN AND
WOMEN, THERE ARE TROPHIES AND A CASH PRIZE.SEE SONNY RAHM, TO ENTER. ALSO
THERE WILL BE BINGO FOR THOSE INTERESTED IN PLAYING. SEE NADAJA BONDY.
CHARMAYNE GOCHENOUR, WILL BE HAVING GAMES FOR THE ADULTS, AND CHILDREN. SO
GET INVOLVED IN SOMTHING AND HAVE FUN.
   WE ARE SELLING FAMILY BUTTONS AT THE TABLE FOR&$1.00 BE SURE TO GET ONE.
AND DON"FORGET TO REGISTER AT THE TABLE, THIS HELPS ME TO KEEP UP WITH
ANY ADDRESS CHANGES, SO EVERYONE GETS THEIR INVITATION NEXT YEAR.WE ALSO
HAVE SOME FREE GIFTS FOR YOU WHEN YOU REGISTER. THER HAS BEEN AN INCREASE IN
THE COST OF THE PICNIC AREA, IT HAS GONE UP TO $75.00 , SO WE ARE HAVING A
SPECIAL RAFFLE TO PAY FOR THE PARK. THERE ARE OVER 25 PRIZES FOR ADULTS
OR CHILDREN SOOEVREYONE CAN BUY A TICKET AND WIN. MOST OF ALL LET'S NOT FORGET
THE AUCTION, THIS IS WHAT PAYS FOR THE NEXT REUNION, SO BE SURE AND LOOK
OVER THE TABLE AND BID ON SOMTHING.
   TODAY WE HONOR OUR SENIOR WOODBURY, LUELLA HINDS, SHE TURNED 84 YEARS YOUNG ON
JUNE 18th. ,SO BE SURE TO STOP AND SAY HI TO HER.I WISH TO THANK ALL OF THE
PEOPLE WHO HAVE MADE THIS YEARS REUNION A SUCCESS. SONNY & MARLENE RAHM,
CHARMAYNE GOCHENOUR, NADAJA BONDY, BABE & CECIL OSENBAUGH, AND RAYMOND WOODBURY
OUR FAMILY HISTORIAN. WITHOUT ALL OF THEM THIS WOULD NOT BE POSSIBLE. AND
TO ALL OF YOU WHO CAME TODAY, THANK YOU!!!
   SO NOW LET'S JUST HAVE FUN....FUN.... FUN!!!!!!!!

WOODBURY HONORS

TODAY WE HONOR THE MEMORY OF MAUDE FLORENCE WOODBURY(SHANNAWAY).ON AUGUST 12, 1994, SHE WOULD HAVE BEEN 100 YEARS OLD. MAUDE PASSED AWAY ON JULY 7, 1977, AT THE AGE OF 82. MAUDIE IS GREATLY MISSED BY ALL OF US WHO KNEW HER.

MAUDE WAS THE MOTHER OF FIVE CHILDREN, GEARLD & HARRY AUTEN, WHO DIED YOUNG. THEY WERE OF HER FIRST MARRIAGE TO ARRON AUTEN.
OF HER SECOND MARRIAGE TO LOUIS SHANNAWAY WERE BORN THREE CHILDREN. MARY SHANNAWAY, SHE MARRIED ERNEST (PAT) WAGNER,THEY HAD FOUR CHILDREN, GR.CHILDREN. GRT. GR. CHILDREN . THEY LIVE IN NEW PORT,MI.

LOUIS SHANNAWAY , MARRIED TO BARBRA STUARD, THEY HAD SEVEN CHILDREN, GR & GRT GR. CHILDREN. THEY BOTH PASSED AWAY IN 1982,WHERE THEY LIVED IN FLORIDA.

JESSIE SHANNAWAY WAS KILLED IN ACTION DURING WWII, AT AGE OF 21.

LOUIS SR. PASSED AWAY IN 1924, OF INJURIES HE RECIEVED IN WWI.

MAUDIE MARRIED BILL GREEN IN 1935. THEY LIVED IN MONROE, MI. UNTIL HIS DEATH IN 1958.

SO TODAY WE SALUTE ALL OF MAUDES DECENDENTS WHO ARE HERE WITH US TODAY AT OUR CELEBRATION OF FAMILY ON AUGUST 28, 1994.

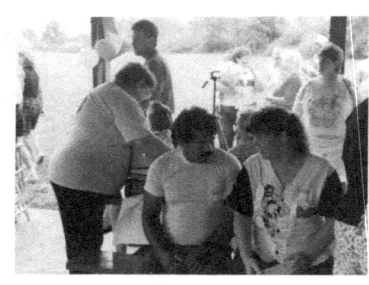

Woodbury

Reunion

1996

WOODBURY
SOUTHERN
REUNION
JULY 13,
1996

March 1, 1996

Luann Velasquez
2531 Tulane Dr.
Cocoa, Florida 32926
Ph #407-690-2256

Hi Cuz,

Well here I am once again. It is only a few months until our first <u>FLORIDA REUNION</u>. I have the Park and Pavilion all lined up for July 13, 1996. I am inclosing a map with the location of the park, and how to get there from all the major roads in the area.

As I mentioned in my first letter, I will need to get from everyone a $10.00 donation to help start this first one. The pavilion is costing me $175.00 for the day. We have a lot planned and from the response it seems like there will be a good turnout. So I think it will be a day filled with lots of good food, fun & family enjoyment.

I am also going to ask you to please give me an R.S.V.P. as soon as possible so I have an idea as to how many of you plan on attending this family reunion? An please include your $10.00. I will give you a receipt in return for your money.

As I said in my first letter, we will have a clown for a few hours that day to do magic tricks and face paintings, we also will have a dunking booth, dart booth, water pistol booth and a duck pond. I will need volunteers for the booths (especially the dunking booth so anyone who fells the need to get wet let me know.) Also don't forget to bring something to be auctioned. And a covered dish, we have so many great cooks in this family it is always a pleasure to try someone else cooking for a change. I am also purchasing gifts to raffle that will be displayed on a table. We will be furnishing hotdogs & hamburgers, but you will need to provided your own beverage (Please no alcoholic beverages, Thanks).

Hope to be hearing from you soon. I'm looking forward to seeing you at the reunion and having an enjoyable day. HOPE YOU CAN ALL COME.

P.S. anyone wanting to donate a small cake for the cake/walk would be greatly appreciated.

Your Cuz;

Luann Velasquez

Luann (Woodbury) Velasquez

Here are a few suggestions as to some of the things we would like to do, And I would like to hear some of your input on these:

(1)	50/50 Raffle	(Y)	(N)
(2)	Bingo	(Y)	(N)
(3)	Horseshoes	(Y)	(N)
(4)	Baseball game men vs. women	(Y)	(N)
(5)	Cake-walk	(Y)	(N)
(6)	Volleyball	(Y)	(N)
(7)	Three-legged race	(Y)	(N)
(8)	Sack Race	(Y)	(N)
(9)	Watermelon seed spitting contest	(Y)	(N)
(10)	Orange or balloon transfer race	(Y)	(N)

Please vote on these and send this portion back to me. We will do as many of these things that time will allow.

Woodbury

Reunion

1998

 WOODBURY REUNION 1998

HI ALL.

Well here we are again, planning for the 1998 WOODBURY REUNION . This year the reunion is being hosted by Raymond Woodbury and his family. I hope everyone will give your help ans support to Raymond as you have me in the past years.

This years reunion will be held on SUNDAY AUGUST 16 th. at the FRATERNAL ORDER OF POLICE HALL in MONROE,MI. It is located on STRASSBURG RD, between DUNBAR and CUSTAR (M-50) RDS. It is a beautiful place to have a reunion as anyone who was there last year can tell you.

Raymond has many fun things planned for this years reunion. There will be a silent auction,a eucre tournament, bingo,horseshose tournament, games for the kiddies and much more.

The main theme of this years reunion is GETTING TO KNOW EACH OTHER AGAIN. The reunion will start at 11:00 am PLEASE TRY TO BE THERE EARLY.Lunch will be served at 1:00 pm. This will give everyone time to get there and time to visit with each other.

At the 1997 WOODBURY REUNION MARY WAGNER became our SENIOR WOODBURY. Mary is the daughter of Maude Woodbury, and is the oldest living member of our clan. Mary is 77years old and lives in Monroe ,Mi with her husband Pat. CONGRATULATIONS MARY!! From all the Woodbury Clan.

Last years reunion was held IN MEMORY to LUELLA HINDS & SONNY RAHM who gave so much to getting the reunion started again .They will be missed by all of the family.

Now for the WOODBURY FAMILY NEWS, I am sad to report that we lost some of our family members this past year. Richard Hinds passed away on March 23,1998, he had been ill with Cancer for the past couple of years. Sonny Rahm passed away Aug.4,1997 of Cancer. Vivian Morris, Grand-daughter of Zenith & Vivian Osenbaugh, and Wilma Fox mother of Darlene Dudley. We send out our sympathy and love to all of their family members.

I would like to send out GET WELL WISHES to all of our family members who have been ill recently. LUANN VELASQUEZ, ZENITH OSENBAUGH,

JAMIE KURTZ, JIMMY HINDS, CHRISTINA LEICHTY, and to all of the rest that I did not hear about, that have been under the weather.

IF YOU ARE INTERESTED I HELPING RAYMOND AT THE REUNION , PLEASE CONTACT HIM . I AM SURE HE WILL APPRECIATE YOUR HELP!

I would like to express my gratitude to everyone who helped me over the years, it would not have been possible without all you. THANKS!!!!
As some of you know I may be moving to Florida this summer, and am not sure if I will make it to this years reunion, but I will be thinking of all of you. Even though I will be in Florida I will be willing to help in any way I can.

DON'T FORGET SUNDAY AUGUST 24 th, THE WOODBURY REUNION.
AT THE F.O.P. HALL IN MONROE, MICHIGAN
STRASSBURG RD (BETWEEN DUNBAR & CUSTAR RDS.

BE THERE AND GET TO KNOW EACH OTHER AGAIN!!!!!!

DIANNA PARKER
ajpajp2@wcnet.org

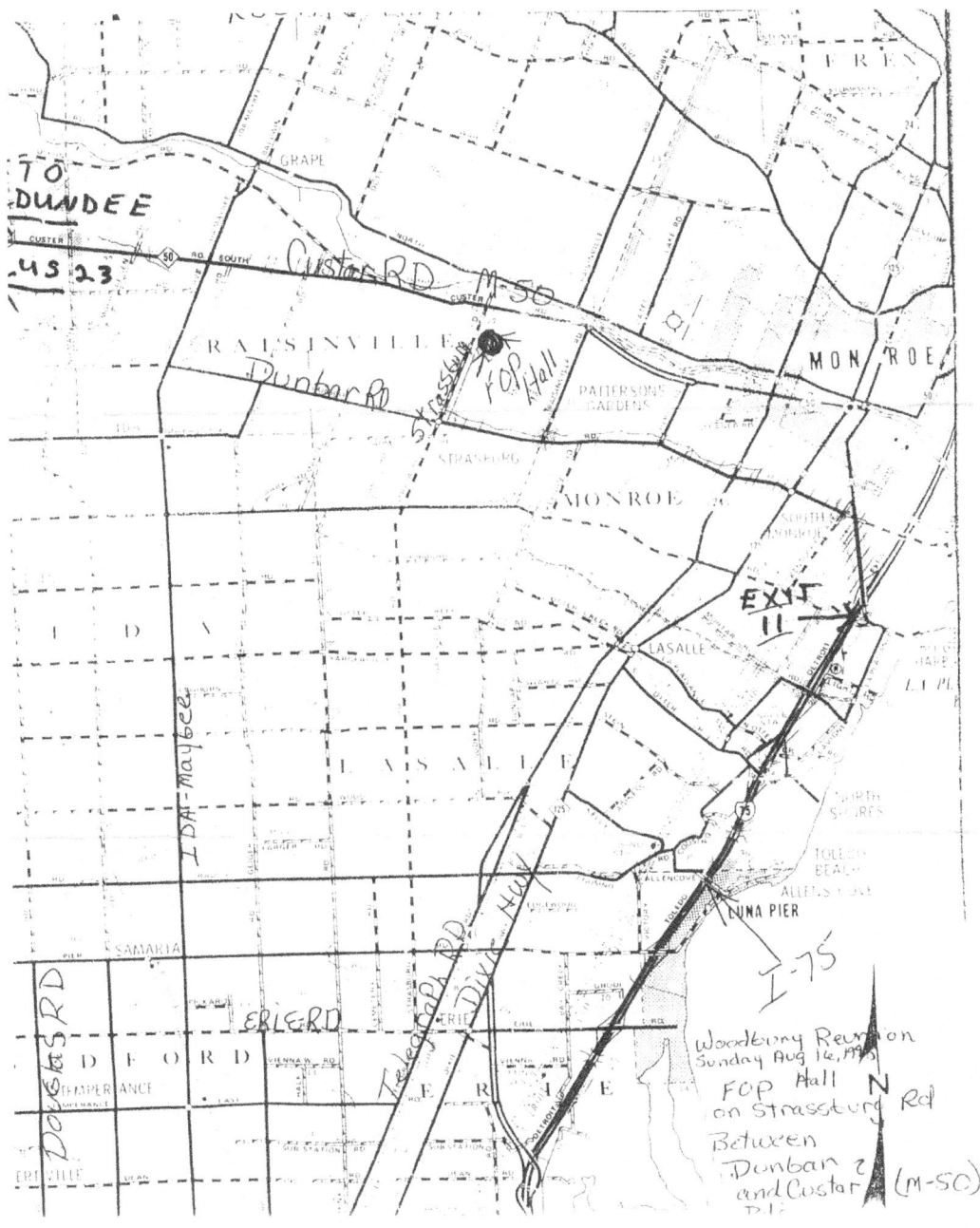

Woodbury Reunion
Sunday Aug 16, 1998
FOP Hall
on Strassburg Rd
Between
Dunban
and Custar (M-50)
Rd

Woodbury

Reunion

2001

Woodbury

WOODBURY & RELATED FAMILY
HEROS

OUR GRATITUDE TO THOSE WHO SERVED
THE COUNTRY

This book is dedicated in memory of
Luann Woodbury Velasquez.

Luann had the idea for this book and started working on it for the Woodbury 2000 celebration but due to her illness she was unable to finish it. I agreed to finish it for her for this the 2001 reunion , but it is her book.

I wish to Thank all who took the time to send me the information to do this book

Dianna Rahm Parker

*Woodbury Hero*s

This is a book about the Woodbury and related family members who have
served our country throughout the years.

The Woodbury family in America starts with John Woodbury born in 1579
in Somerset-shier ,England, who came here in 1624 in the interest of the
Dorchester Company and settled Cape Ann, now know as Gloucester, Mass.
In 1626 John returned to England and later returned and was one of the
origional founders of the town of Salem, Mass. In the 1700's the family
migrated to Maine ,New Hampshire, Vermont and Georgia. In the early
1800's the family began migrating westward to Ohio, Michigan and beyond.

There were many Woodbury's who served in the Revolutionary War, we
have not been able to trace our direct line back to any one person yet.
so our book starts with the first proven ancestor, Daniel Woodbury.

Daniel Woodbury
1791-1878

Daniel was born in Bridport , Vermont in 1791. He married Experience Durkee in Orwell, Vermont on January 10,1810.Daniel was a farmer in Orwell until he enlisted on September 29, 1812 and was mustered in on November 1,1812 in Capt. Benjamin S. Edgerton's Co, 11th Regt.; in Burlington , Vermont

He was at the battle at Sacketts Harbor, and at the battle at Chryslers Farm where he was taken prisoner on November 11,1813. He was held prisoner at Quebec until his release at Chazy, New York in 1814, he then returned to his family in Orwell.

Though there are no pictures of Daniel we can only imagine what he looked like in his uniform. From his military records we know he was 5'10" with a light complexion with sandy hair and blue eyes.

Daniel and his family moved from Vermont to Ohio in 1817 where he settled in Portage County. In the late 1840's the family moved to Michigan, first Blissfield, then taking up residence in Monroe, County

Daniel was the father of 14 children and a farmer in Whiteford Center, Michigan until his death on August 8,1878.

Daniel recieved a pension of $8.00 a month starting on February 14,1871.

His son Joseph Woodbury buried Daniel, but it is unknown where he is buried. His coffin was purchased from Bennett & Schroeder Undertakers, 218 Summit Street , Toledo, Ohio for 18 dollars.

U.S. Infantryman, 1812

This private soldier, wearing the blue uniform, is biting off a cartridge prior to loading his Springfield musket. For comfort, he has pushed his cartridge box, or cartouche, behind his back, while over his white cross belts can be seen the straps of his knapsack on his back. The belts of his canteen and cloth haversack, containing his rations, hang on his left hip. The regular infantry of both armies dressed for display rather than utility.

STATE OF VERMONT
OFFICE OF THE ADJUTANT GENERAL
~~XAXWXXXNXXQNXXWXNXXXXXXXVERXXXXXXXXXXX~~
Montpelier, Vt. 05602
.................30 October 1985..........

I Hereby Certify that the following is a correct transcript from the records in this office regarding the following soldier who served in the WAR OF 1812

Woodbury, Daniel

Enlisted Nov 1, 1812 in Capt. Benjamin S. Edgerton's Co, 11th Regt.; on Pay Roll for September and October, 1812 and January and February, 1813; was at the battle of Chrystler's Farm Nov 11, 1813 and was reported missing after the battle.

Elwin W. Dean
ELWIN W. DEAN
FOR: DONALD E. EDWARDS
The Adjutant General

3M 3/80

DECLARATION FOR PENSION.

WAR OF 1812.

State of _Michigan_ }
County of _Lenawee_ } ss.

On this _20th_ day of _April_ A. D. 187_1_, personally appeared before me, _Clerk_ of the _Circuit_ Court, a court of record, within and for the County and State aforesaid, _Daniel Woodbury_ aged _80_ years, a resident of _Whiteford_, county of _Monroe_ State of _Michigan_ who being duly sworn according to law, declares that he is married, that his wife's name was _Experience Durkee_ to whom he was married, at _Orville Vt_ on the _6th_ day of _January_ 18_10_. That he served the full term of sixty days, in the _Military_ service of the United States in the war of 1812. That he is the identical _Daniel Woodbury_ who _Volunteered_ in Captain _Adjutants_ Company, _11_ Regiment _Col. Upham_ Brigade, _Gen Wilkins_ Division, of _U.S. Regulars_ at _Burlington Vt_ in the fall _of_ 1812, and was honorably discharged at _Burlington_ on the _____ day of _____ 18_14_. _That he was in Sackette Harbor during summer of 1813, and was taken prisoner at Williamsbury Canada in an engagement and kept prisoner at Quebic till May 1814 when he was exchanged at Plattsburg or near there. He had a furlough from Col. Bette then commanding he e_

and further that in no time during the late Rebellion against the authority of the United States did I adhere to the cause of the enemies of the United States Government, neither give them aid or comfort, nor exercised the functions of any office whatsoever under any authority or pretended authority in hostility to the United States. I further swear that I will support the Constitution of the United States, that I am not in receipt of a Pension under any previous act.

This declaration is made for the purpose of being placed on the Pension Roll of the United States under the provision of the act approved February 14th, 1871, and I hereby constitute and appoint, with full power of substitution and revocation, _R. B. Robins Adrian Mich etc._ my true and lawful attorney to prosecute this claim. My Post Office Address is _Whiteford, Carlton_ County of _Monroe_ State of _Michigan_ and that my residence is _Whiteford, Monroe W._

ATTEST.
H. Stearns
_____   _Daniel Woodbury_
                                                        Applicant.

Sworn to, subscribed and acknowledged before me the day and year first above written ; and also personally appeared _Almond L. Blis_ and _Willard S._ residents of the _County_ of _Lenawee_ in the State of _Michigan_ persons whom I certify to be respectable and entitled to credit, and who being duly sworn, say that they were present and saw _Daniel Woodbury_ to the foregoing declaration : and they further swear that they have every reason to believe from the appearance of the applicant and their acquaintance with him that he is the identical person he represents himself to be, and they know that at no time during the Rebellion against the authority of the United States did he adhere to the cause of the enemies of the Government, neither give them aid or comfort, nor exercised the functions of any office whatsoever under any authority or pretended authority in hostility to the United States, and that they reside as above stated, and that they have no interest in the prosecution of this claim.

[Two witnesses when Mark is made.]

_____   _Almond L. Blis_
_____   _Willard Stearns_

Sworn to and subscribed before me, this _20_ day of _April_ A. D., 187_1_ and I hereby certify that I have no interest, direct or indirect, in the prosecution of this claim. I further certify, that the foregoing declaration and joint affidavit, were fully made known to and explained to the applicant and witnesses before swearing, including the words _Volunteer in the Myron E Knight_ erased, and the words _on land_ _Willard Stearns_ added.

_____
Clerk OF THE _Circuit_ COURT.

WAR OF 1812

ACT FEBRUARY 14, 1871.

1640 Dec 7 920

BRIEF OF CLAIM FOR A SURVIVOR'S PENSION

in the case of *Daniel Woodbury*

of Captain *Egerton, Bliss & Adjutant* Company, Colonel *11th U.S. Infty* Reg't.

Residence; *Monroe Co, Michigan*

POST OFFICE ADDRESS:

Whiteford Centre, Monroe Co, Michigan

Enlisted *29 Sept* , 18 *12*, Present discharged *May 11* , 18 *14*

Served afterward from _____ , 18__ , to _____ , 18__

in Captain _____ Company, Colonel _____ Reg't.

Declaration and identification in due form, filed *April 29* , 18 *71.*

SERVICE FOR SIXTY DAYS, SHOWN AS FOLLOWS:

*Report from Adjutant General shows that Daniel
Woodbury served in Capt. Benj. S Egerton's Capt. Bliss
and Capt. Adjutant Co's from 29 Sept 1812 to 11th May 1814,
Prisoner of War, exchanged and received at Chazy
by Maj. Churchill, May 11 1814, No further information.*

Length of service, *590* days.

Claimant declares he is not a pensioner under any previous act. Name not on list of pensioners

Loyalty, claimant's averment and testimony of *A. L. Bliss + Milliard Stearns*

Oath to support the Constitution of the United States *subscribed.* ✓

Admitted *Nov. 9* , 187*1*, to a pension of eight dollars per month, from

February 14, 1871.

D. B. Robbins, atty;
*Adrian
Michigan*

Jno Gorman , Ex'r.
App'd. *F. D. Yeager*
Reviewer.

Sacketts Harbor
Attacked

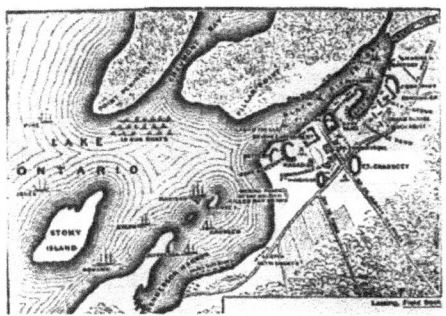

On May 27, 1813, the British attack Sacketts Harbor. The British force is repulsed after a difficult battle.

Look at great battles of the war in greater detail

explore
History
CAUSES
TIMELINE
BATTLES
PEOPLE
AFTERMATH

expand
your Knowledge
ATLAS
QUIZ
TOUR

exchange
Information
FORUM
LINKS
FEEDBACK

in the United States | in Canada

Battle of Crysler's Farm

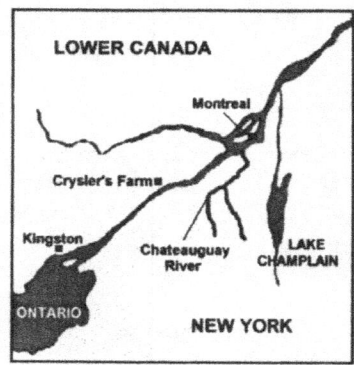

The St. Lawrence Region
Source: Team 22916

American Major General James Wilkinson arrived at the naval base at Sackett's Harbor in early October, 1813. His plan was to strike at Montreal by traveling down the St. Lawrence River, while Major General

David Woodbury
1820-1894

David Woodbury was born on October 4,1820 in Portage County, Ohio to Daniel & Experience Woodbury. He was the father of our ancestor John Milton Woodbury.
David served with the Union Army during the Civil War not once but twice.
He enlisted in Company H of the 15th. Michigan Infantry on March 25, 1861 in Monroe, Michigan. He served as a private in Captain John Adams Company. He was Discharged with a Surgeons Certification of Disability, at Cornith, Mississippi on September 13, 1862. David enlisted the second time , at the age of 36 in Company G of the 13th regiment of the Michigan Infantry and was mustered in at Grand Rapids, Michigan on January 5,1864.He served at Lookout Mountain and became ill with Rheumatisim and a Kidney complaint while getting timber for the Chattanooga Bridge. David spent much of the time in the hospital sick until his discharge August 13,1865
David was married many times and was the father of 6 children David was a laborer and a farmer until his death in Adrain , Michigan on April9, 1994.He is buried in Oakwood Cemetary in Adrain. On April 12, 1894. Davids wife Susan Weatherby Woodbury applied for a widows pension .They were married on July 5,1887 in Blissfield, Michigan and at his death they lived at 76 Erie Street in Adrain. She recieved an $8.00 a month until September 4,1901 when the pension was dropped. David's burial expenses were paid by his brother Joseph Woodbury of Whiteford Center , Michigan.

Pension Application

VOLUNTEER ENLISTMENT.

STATE OF MICHIGAN,

City
Town of *Detroit* — County of *Wayne*

I, *David Woodbury* born in *Ravenna* in the State of *Ohio* aged *46* years, and by occupation a *Farmer* Do Hereby Acknowledge to have volunteered this *31st* day of *December* 186_,
to serve as a SOLDIER IN THE ARMY OF THE UNITED STATES OF AMERICA for the period of THREE YEARS, unless sooner discharged by proper authority. Do also agree to accept such bounty, pay, rations and clothing, as are, or may be, established by law for volunteers. And I, *David Woodbury* do solemnly swear, that I will bear true faith and allegiance to the UNITED STATES OF AMERICA, and that I will serve them honestly and faithfully against all their enemies or opposers whomsoever; and that I will observe and obey the orders of the President of the United States, and the orders of the officers appointed over me, according to the Rules and Articles of War.

Sworn and subscribed to, at *Detroit*
this *31st* day of *Decr* 1863

Before *Geo. W. Robinson*
Notary Public

his
David X Woodbury
mark

I CERTIFY, ON HONOR, That I have carefully examined the above named volunteer, agreeably to the General Regulations of the Army, and that in my opinion he is free from all bodily defects and mental infirmity, which would, in any way, disqualify him from performing the duties of a soldier.

Geo. Landon
Examining Surgeon.

I CERTIFY, ON HONOR, That I have minutely inspected the Volunteer,_____ _____ previously to his enlistment, and that he was entirely sober when enlisted; that, to the best of my judgment and belief, he is of lawful age; and that, in accepting him as duly qualified to perform the duties of an able-bodied soldier, I have strictly observed the Regulations which govern the recruiting service. This soldier has *blue* eyes, *brown* hair, *fair* complexion, is *5* feet *7 1/2* inches high.

_____Regiment of Michigan Volunteers. (Infantry,)
Recruiting Officer.

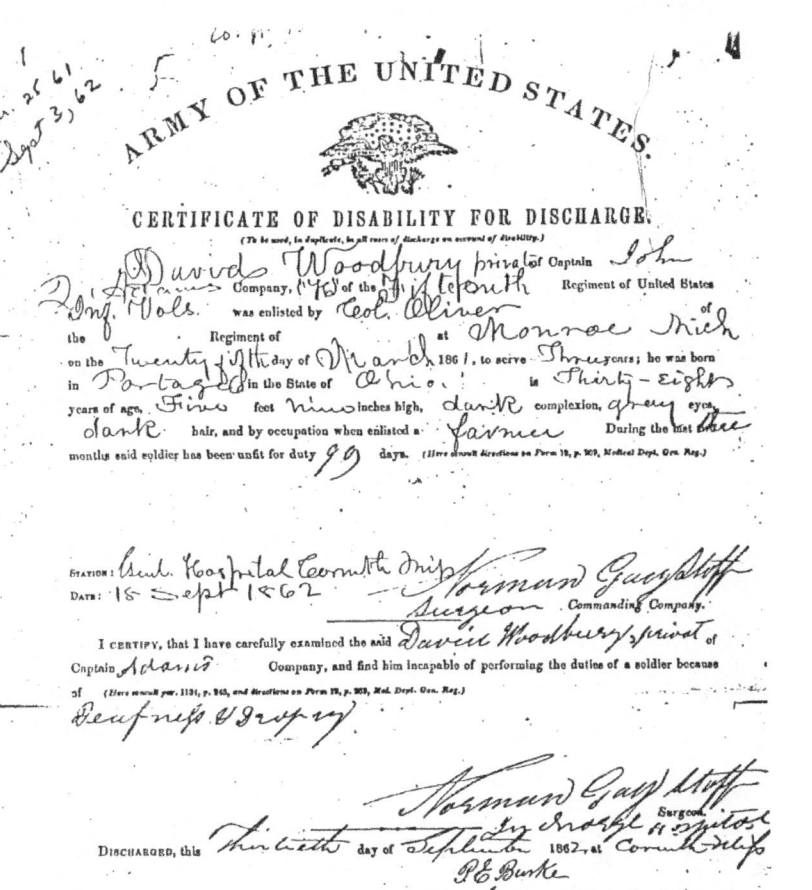

ARMY OF THE UNITED STATES.

CERTIFICATE OF DISABILITY FOR DISCHARGE.

(To be used, in duplicate, in all cases of discharge on account of disability.)

David Woodbury private of Captain John
Adams Company, "K" of the Fifteenth Regiment of United States
Inf. Vols. was enlisted by Col. Oliver at Monroe Mich
the Regiment of on the Twenty fifth day of March 1861, to serve Three years; he was born
in Portage in the State of Ohio, is Thirty-Eight
years of age, Five feet nine inches high, dark complexion, grey eyes,
dark hair, and by occupation when enlisted a farmer During the last three
months said soldier has been unfit for duty 90 days. (Here insert directions on Form 19, p. 209, Medical Dept. Gen. Reg.)

STATION: Genl. Hospital Corinth Miss   Norman Gay Stoff
DATE: 18 Sept 1862   Surgeon   Commanding Company.

I CERTIFY, that I have carefully examined the said David Woodbury, private of
Captain Adams Company, and find him incapable of performing the duties of a soldier because
of (Here insert par. 1131, p. 243, and directions on Form 19, p. 209, Mel. Dept. Gen. Reg.)

Deafness & Dropsy

                                    Norman Gay Stoff
                                          Surgeon.
                                    In charge Hospital
DISCHARGED, this Thirtieth day of September 1862, at Corinth Miss
                        P. E. Burke
                        Col. 14 Wis. Vols. Commanding the Post.

NOTE 1.—When a probable case for pension, special care must be taken to state the degree of disability.
NOTE 2.—The place where the soldier desires to be addressed may be here added.
        Town—   County—   State—

[GOVT. PRINT. OFF., Oct., 1861.]   (DUPLICATE.)   15

Adjutant General's Office,

Washington, D. C.

May 2 . 1866.

Sir:

I have the honor to acknowledge the receipt from your Office of application for Pension No. 91,693, and to return it herewith, with such information as is furnished by the files of this Office.

It appears from the Rolls on file in this Office, that David Woodbury was enrolled on the 31st day of Dec., 1863, at Detroit in Co. "G", 13th Regiment of Mich Volunteers, to serve 3 years, or during the war, and mustered into service as a Rect on the 5th day of Jan. 1864, at Grand Rapids Mich, in Co. "G", 13th Regiment of Mich Volunteers, to serve 3 years, or during the war. On the Muster Roll of Co. "G" of that Regiment, for the months of dated July 25 1865, he is reported a Priv't - Abst sick at Louisville Ky. June 6th/65 - has Des. List - no discharge furnished at Muster out of organization. (See individual M. O. Roll of soldier.) Mustd. out Aug. 17th/65, in accordance with instructions no 2 from the Dept date May 3/65, reason of sickness not stated. No further evidence of disability.

I am, Sir, very respectfully,

Your obedient servant,

Geo. D. Buck
Assistant Adjutant General.

The Commissioner of Pensions,
Washington D. C.

Memoranda:

Name of applicant

Address

13

J. C. Hull

Adjutant General's Office,

Washington, D. C., August 26th, 1876

Sir:

I have the honor to acknowledge the receipt from your Office of application for Pension No. 91.693_____, and to return it herewith, with such information as is furnished by the files of this Office.

It appears from the Rolls on file in this Office that David Woodbury_____ was enrolled on the _____ 31st day of _____ Dec. _____, 1863, at Detroit Mich, in Co. "G", 13th Regiment of Michigan_____ Volunteers, to serve ___3___ years or during the war, and mustered into service as a Recruit_____ on the ___5th___ day of ___Jany___, 1864, at Detroit Mich._____, in Co. "A", 19th Regiment of Michigan_____ Volunteers, to serve ___3___ years, or during the war. On the Muster Roll of Co "A", of that Regiment, for the months of Jany & Feby Mar & April (4 months muster), 1864, he is reported Absent on Det. service in Harden Square May & June July & Aug 64, present for duty. Sept & Oct 64 roll not on file Nov & Dec 64 left sick at Chattanooga Oct 26/64, same report to April 30/65. May & June 65 sick in Louisville Ky June 18/65 He was admitted to No 2 G. H. Lookout Mt. near Chattanooga, Tenn, Oct 6th 64, with Chr. Rheumatism, and was transferred April 12th 65, entered No. 1 G. H. Nashville, Tenn April 18th 1865, with Chr. Rheumatism and was transferred May 4th 1865, entered Crittenden G. H. Louisville, Ky., May 4th 1865 with Chr. Rheumatism, and was transferred June 10 1865, entered from (No. 7 J G. H. Louisville Ky June 13/65 with Chr. Rheumatism, and was transferred June 22 1865, entered Harper G. H. Detroit Mich, June 27 1865 with Chr. Rheumatism, and returned to duty July 28 1865. Countries out on Ind' roll August 14th 1865 at Harper Gen. Hosp. Detroit Mich. No Record of alleged injury. (He was at home on Det. furlough in Mar. 64, arrived at Chattanooga Tenn April 20/64)

I am, sir, very respectfully,

___13___ Your obedient servant,

Assistant Adjutant General.

EDWIN BOWERS

Edwin was the son of Polly (Woodbury) & Eleazer Bowers was born in 1843. He served with the Union forces in Company H of the 15th Michigan Infantry during the Civil War. He was discharged March 22,1865. He lived in Summerfield Twsp. Michigan.

Gilbert Bosom
1845- 1888

Gilbert Bosom was born in 1845 to Joseph and Julia (Bodet) Bosom in Erie Michigan. He married Rosalie Bernard on December 26,1860 in Whiteford Twsp. Michigan. Gilbert enlisted as a private in the Union Army I Company 13th.Michigan Infantry at Jackson, Michigan on December 31,1863. He was mustered out on July 25,1865 at Louisville, Kentucky. Gilbert filed for an Invalid Pension on August 5,1887. Rosa filed for a widows pension on August 5,1888. After the war he returned to Blissfield where he worked as a laborer for Lewis Monroe. He then moved to Reed City, Michigan .Gilbert died June 6,1888 and is buried in Wellington , Michigan. He was the father of Joseph, and 1/2 brother of John Milton Woodbury.

Name of Regiment	Date of Organization	Muster Date	Regiment Type
Michigan 13th Infantry Regiment	17 January 1862	25 July 1865	Infantry
Officers Killed or Mortally Wounded	Officers Died of Disease or Accident	Enlisted Killed or Mortally Wounded	Enlisted Died of Disease or Accident
4	2	68	314

List of Soldiers

Regimental History

Battles Fought
Battle at Iuka, Mississippi
Battle on 29 March 1862
Battle at Corinth, Mississippi on 19 May 1862
Battle at Corinth, Mississippi on 14 June 1862
Battle at Stevenson, Alabama on 26 August 1862
Battle at Near Stevenson, Alabama on 01 September 1862
Battle at Tyree Springs, Tennessee on 07 September 1862
Battle at Near Springfield, Missouri on 08 October 1862
Battle at Perryville, Kentucky on 08 October 1862
Battle at Gallatin, Tennessee on 16 November 1862
Battle on 15 December 1862
Battle at Stones River, Tennessee on 29 December 1862
Battle at Stones River, Tennessee on 31 December 1862
Battle at Stones River, Tennessee on 02 January 1863
Battle at Stones River, Tennessee on 15 January 1863
Battle on 20 June 1863
Battle on 12 July 1863
Battle at Chickamauga, Georgia on 19 September 1863
Battle at Chickamauga, Georgia on 20 September 1863
Battle at Crawfish Springs, Georgia on 20 September 1863
Battle at Chattanooga, Tennessee on 26 September 1863
Battle at Milledgeville, Georgia on 23 November 1864
Battle at Milledgeville, Georgia on 25 November 1864
Battle at Savannah, Georgia on 12 December 1864
Battle at Taken To Hospital Indiana Savannah, Georgia on 28 December 1864
Battle at Aiken, South Carolina on 09 February 1865
Battle at On March Through South Carolina on 09 February 1865
Battle on 01 March 1865
Battle at Catawaba River, North Carolina on 01 March 1865
Battle on 04 March 1865
Battle on 05 March 1865
Battle on 07 March 1865
Battle at Kinston, North Carolina on 08 March 1865
Battle at Near Rockingham, South Carolina on 08 March 1865
Battle on 09 March 1865
Battle on 10 March 1865
Battle at North Carolina on 10 March 1865
Battle at Bentonville, North Carolina on 19 March 1865
Battle at Goldsboro, North Carolina on 24 March 1865
Battle on 27 March 1865
Battle at Goldsboro, North Carolina on 02 April 1865
Battle on 19 April 1865
Battle at Goldsboro, North Carolina on 23 April 1865

ELI WOODBURY
1839-1915

   Eli Woodbury was born to Daniel and Experience Woodbury in 1839 in
Portage County Ohio. On March 31,1862 at Whiteford, Michigan he
enlisted in the Union forces in Company H 15th Michigan Infantry. Eli was
discharged at Coddsboro, North Carolina on April 7,1865.
   Eli was a farmer in Deerfield, Michigan, and married Rosaltha Black on
October 16,1866 in Whiteford , Michigan. Eli died on September 4,1915 and
is buried in Blissfield Cemetary in Blissfield , Michigan. Eli and Rosa had
no children.

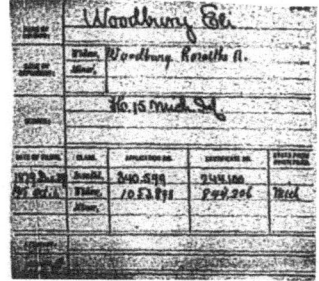

Lucas Bosom
1843- 1919

Lucas Bosom was born on October 19,1843 in Erie, Michigan to Joseph and Julia((Bodet) Bosom. He married Sara J Barry in about 1867 in Blissfield, Mi. At the age of 19 he enlisted in the Union Army on March 22,1863 at Blissfield, as a private in L Company 1st. Michigan Engineers and Mechanics. He was discharged on June 12,1865 at Camp Chase in Ohio as a 1Cl.privite. Luke filed for his Invalid Pension in August 1912. Sarah filed for a widows pension on August 12,1919.

After the war Luke returned to Blissfield where he worked for Lewis Monroe as a laborer. In the 1870's He moved to West Branch, Michigan and on March 16,1888 he received Homestead land in Reed City, Michigan, where he moved with his family and became a farmer. Luke died on July 26,1919 in West Branch, and is buried there. He was the father of six children and the 1/2 brother of John Milton Woodbury

Lewis A. Monroe
1825 - 1908

Lewis Monroe was born on March 5, 1825 in England to Merrick and Susan Monroe.

Lewis served in the Union Army in L Company , Michigan 1st Engineers Regiment He enlisted on June 23,1863 in Adrian, Michigan. He was mustered out on September 22,1865 in Nashville , Tennessee. After the war Lewis returned to Adrian where he had a clock repair shop He also invented a special saw for cutting wood . He hired many others in the family to cut wood for him. He married Mary Lucinda Rowe on February 18, 1902 in Adrian. Lewis died March 6.1908 in Jasper, Michigan. Lewis was possibly the uncle of John Milton Woodbury.

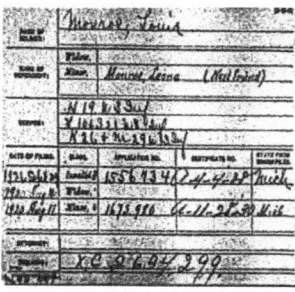

61st Illinois Infantry, 1st Michigan Engineers and 12th Indiana Cavalry.

A train bearing these troops from Stevenson to Murfreesboro was fired into near Christiana and it became necessary for the detachment to disembark and repair the road.

Even then the progress of the train was very slow and when within 6 miles of Murfreesboro it became apparent that it would have to be abandoned and an attempt made to cut a way out, as by this time it was wholly surrounded.

After a desperate fight about 8 p. m. the Federals managed to break through the enemy's line, but only after losing 85 men of the 61st Ill., including the colonel, the whole detachment of engineers and the larger portion of the 30 men of the 12th Ind. cavalry.

Most of the men were captured.

Source: The Union Army, vol. 6, p. 626

Name of Regiment	Date of Organization	Muster Date	Regiment Type
Michigan 1st Engineers Regiment	29 October 1861	22 September 1865	Engineers

Officers Killed or Mortally Wounded	Officers Died of Disease or Accident	Enlisted Killed or Mortally Wounded	Enlisted Died of Disease or Accident
1	0	12	341

List of Soldiers

Regimental History

Battles Fought
Battle at Bridgeport, Alabama
Battle at Elk River, Tennessee
Battle at Green River
Battle at Mill Springs, Kentucky
Battle at On Nashville And Chattanooga, RR
Battle at Savannah, Georgia
Battle at South Edisto River
Battle at Stones River, Tennessee
Battle on 01 May 1862
Battle at Between Huntsville, Alabama And War Trace, Tennessee on 08 May 1862
Battle on 16 May 1862
Battle at Between Huntsville, Alabama And War Trace, Tennessee on 20 May 1862
Battle at Stevenson, Alabama on 17 August 1862
Battle on 19 August 1862
Battle at Munfordsville, Kentucky on 16 September 1862
Battle at Chaplin Hills, Kentucky on 08 October 1862

Battle at Perryville, Kentucky on 08 October 1862
Battle at Chaplin Hills, Kentucky on 09 October 1862
Battle on 24 November 1862
Battle at Munfordsville, Kentucky on 15 December 1862
Battle at Lavergne, Tennessee on 01 January 1863
Battle at Nashville, Tennessee on 01 January 1863
Battle at Murfreesboro, Tennessee on 29 June 1863
Battle on 15 August 1863
Battle on 08 October 1863
Battle at Tullahoma, Tennessee on 15 October 1863
Battle on 23 October 1863
Battle on 15 February 1864
Battle on 03 March 1864
Battle on 16 March 1864
Battle at Brownsboro on 01 May 1864
Battle on 18 August 1864
Battle on 13 October 1864
Battle on 15 October 1864
Battle at Big Shanty, Georgia on 16 October 1864
Battle at Kingston, Georgia on 29 October 1864
Battle at Louisville, Georgia on 30 November 1864
Battle at Savannah, Georgia on 10 December 1864
Battle at Murfreesboro, Tennessee on 15 December 1864
Battle at Murfreesboro, Tennessee on 16 December 1864
Battle at On March on 20 February 1865
Battle at Fayetteville, North Carolina on 14 March 1865
Battle at Bentonville, North Carolina on 20 March 1865
Battle on 26 March 1865
Battle on 12 April 1865

Albert Woodbury
1824-1901

Albert was born on September 24, 1824 in Portage County, Ohio to Daniel and Experience Woodbury. He married Eliza Reed on December 22, 1846 in Franklin County, Ohio. During the Civil War he enlisted in Company E 67th. Ohio Infantry at Whiteford, Michigan on November 26, 1861, at 37 years old. Albert was discharged on disability July 3, 1963 at Columbus, Ohio. Albert filed for his invalid pension on February 7, 1880. Albert was the father of 6 children and a farmer in Whiteford Center, Michigan. Eliza died on March 15, 1901. Albert married Dinah Montro on May 1, 1891. Albert and Eliza are buried in Whiteford Union Cemetery.

Name of Regiment	Date of Organization	Muster Date	Regiment Type
Ohio 67th Infantry Regiment	01 December 1861	07 December 1865	Infantry

Officers Killed or Mortally Wounded	Officers Died of Disease or Accident	Enlisted Killed or Mortally Wounded	Enlisted Died of Disease or Accident
11	1	131	150

List of Soldiers

Regimental History

Battles Fought
Battle at Bermuda Hundred, Virginia
Battle at Near Richmond, Virginia
Battle at Kearnestown, Virginia on 23 March 1862
Battle at Kearnstown, Virginia on 23 March 1862
Battle at Strasburg, Virginia on 15 May 1862
Battle at Harrison's Landing, Virginia on 04 July 1862
Battle at Harrison's Landing, Virginia on 16 July 1862
Battle at Fort Wagner, South Carolina on 18 July 1863
Battle on 26 July 1863
Battle at Fort Wagner, South Carolina on 07 August 1863
Battle at Morris Island, South Carolina on 21 August 1863
Battle at Wilmington Island, Georgia on 22 February 1864
Battle at Chester Station, Virginia on 09 May 1864
Battle at Chester Station, Virginia on 10 May 1864
Battle at Ware Bottom Church, Virginia on 17 May 1864
Battle at Bermuda Hundred, Virginia on 20 May 1864

Lyman Woodbury
1832 - 1903

Lyman Woodbury was born on July1,1832 in Portage County Ohio to Daniel and Experience Woodbury. He married Margaret Halmony on November 11,1853. During the Civil War at the age of 32, he enlisted in K Company 18th. Michigan Infantry on January 30, 1864,and joined the regiment at Nashville, Tennessee on March 2, 1864, he was in the battles at Decatur, Courtland and Athens ,Alabama. Lyman was discharged on June 25,1865 at Louisville ,Kentucky.

Lyman was the father of 5 children and a framer in Whiteford Center, Michigan. He died January 14,1903 in Blissfield, Michigan. Lymans wife Margaret filed for a widows pension on July 19,1903. He and his wife are buried in Blissfield Cemetary.

Name of Regiment	Date of Organization	Muster Date	Regiment Type
Michigan 18th Infantry Regiment	26 August 1862	26 June 1865	Infantry

Officers Killed or Mortally Wounded	Officers Died of Disease or Accident	Enlisted Killed or Mortally Wounded	Enlisted Died of Disease or Accident
0	0	18	293

List of Soldiers

Regimental History

Battles Fought
Battle at Snow's Pond, Kentucky on 15 September 1862
Battle at Snow's Pond, Kentucky on 23 September 1862
Battle on 25 September 1862
Battle at Snow's Pond, Kentucky on 25 September 1862
Battle on 15 October 1862
Battle on 30 January 1863
Battle at Danville, Kentucky on 24 March 1863
Battle on 04 August 1863
Battle at Nashville, Tennessee on 12 August 1863
Battle at Nashville, Tennessee on 13 August 1863
Battle at Decatur, Alabama on 24 June 1864
Battle at Courtland, Alabama on 27 July 1864
Battle at Athens, Alabama on 24 September 1864
Battle at Decatur, Alabama on 03 January 1865
Battle on 22 April 1865

Louis Shanaway Sr.
1839-1914

Louis Shanaway Sr. was born on September 12,1839 in Montreal, Canada to Leander and Mary Ann (Gonyea) Chenevare. He married Mary Kane in Monroe, Michigan on August 16, 1865. They had 13 children.

Louis enlisted on September 5,1861 in Lucas County, Oh and was mustered in as a private in Captian Wilber Staffords ,Company H,14th.Regiment Ohio Volunteer Infantry. Louis was wounded in the calf of his leg at the engagement at Chickamunga ,Georgia. He was hospitalized for some time , but as soon as he was able he returned to his regiment until the end of the war. he was discharged September 12, 1864 at Atlanta, Ga. Louis died December 30, 1914 in Monroe, Michigan and is buried in St. Joseph Cemetary.

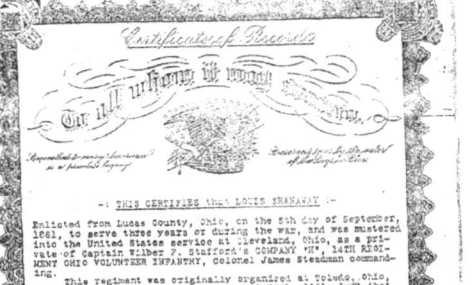

Certificate of Record

On all whom it may

-: THIS CERTIFIES that LOUIS SHANAWAY :-

Enlisted from Lucas County, Ohio, on the 5th day of September, 1861, to serve three years or during the war, and was mustered into the United States service at Cleveland, Ohio, as a private of Captain Wilber F. Stafford's COMPANY "H", 14TH REGIMENT OHIO VOLUNTEER INFANTRY, Colonel James Steadman commanding.

This regiment was originally organized at Toledo, Ohio, for three months service, and on April 28th, 1861, left that city for Camp Taylor, near Cleveland, where a regimental organization was formed with the following field officers, viz:- Jas. Steadman, Colonel; George P. Este, Lt-Col.; Paul Edwards, Major. The regiment remained at Camp Taylor, performing drill and discipline duty until May 22nd, 1861, when it moved to Columbus, where it received arms and accoutrements, and left the same day for Marietta, where it occupied Camp Putnam, where it remained until May 27th, when it was ordered to the front. It later took part in the battles at Phillippi, Laurel Hill, and Carricks Ford, W. Va., at all times performing gallant duty.

The FOURTEENTH OHIO, for three years' service, was organized at Toledo, from August 14th to September 5th, 1861, and was mustered into the service under the same field officers who had commanded the three months regiment. Soon after its reorganization, it moved to Cincinnati, thence across the Ohio River to Covington, Ky., and from there to Lexington and Frankfort. Afterward moved to Nicholasville, and established a camp of rendezvous, where for three weeks it was engaged in daily drill, and was thoroughly disciplined, after which it moved to Camp Dick Robinson, and while there a number of loyal Tennesseeans crawled through the Confederate lines and joined the Union forces. Among these brave men were United States Senator Andrew Johnson, afterward Vice-President and President of the United States, and Horace Maynard, Congressman, both of whom were at that time on their way to Washington. Later the regiment was assigned to the 3rd Brigade, 3rd Division, 14th Corps, Army of the Cumberland, and during its service took part in the following engagements, viz:- Wild Cat, Will Springs Ky.; Shiloh or Pittsburg Landing, Tenn.; Siege of Corinth, Miss.; Perryville or Chapin Hill, Ky.; Nolensville or Knob Gap, Stone River or Murgfreesboro, Hoover's Gap, Tenn.; Chickamauga, Ga.; Orchard Knob, Lookout Mountain, Mission Ridge, Tenn.; Ringgold, Dalton, Resaca, Kenesaw Mountain, Peach Tree Creek, Utoy Creek, Siege of Atlanta, Jonesboro, Lovejoy Station, March to the Sea, Averasboro, Bentonville, Goldsboro, N. C., and a number of minor engagements and skirmishes. After the surrender of Johnston to Sherman at Bennet House, the regiment marched by way of Richmond, Va., to Washington, D. C., where it took part in the Grand Review, on the 23rd of May, 1865, afterward performing duty in Virginia and Kentucky, until ordered home for muster out and final discharge. The regiment at all times performed gallant duty and lost 322 by death while in the service.

The said Louis Shanaway was wounded during the engagement of Chickamauga in the calf of the leg. He was sent to the Hospital, where he remained for some time. As soon as he was able he rejoined his regiment and served with it until the end of the war. He was at all times with his command, except while in hospital, rendering gallant and meritorious service on all occasions, and achieved an enviable record for bravery in action and soldierly bearing at all times, whether in camp, on the march or on the field of battle.

He received a FINAL HONORABLE DISCHARGE at Atlanta, Ga.,

(Continued.)

Compiled from Official Authentic Sources by the
Soldiers & Sailors
Historical & Benevolent Society.
In testimony whereof I have under set
my hand and cause to be affixed the
seal of the Society.
Done at Washington, D. C. this 23rd day
of April, A.D. 190

№ 101141

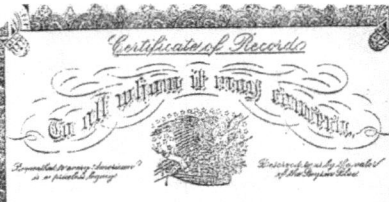

To all whom it may concern

Record No. 101141 Concluded.

on the 22nd day of September, 1864, by reason of close of war.

He was born in Montreal, Canada, on the 12th of September, 1839; was united in marriage to Mary Kane, at Monroe, Michigan, on the 16th day of August, 1865; Rev. Eton Jose performing the ceremony in St. Mary's Catholic Church. From this union were born the following children, viz:- Lewis L., Richard L., Lucile, William, Benjamin, Lewis F., Daniel, Florence, Jessie, Lewis J., Lewis, Emma, Mary.

He is an active and honored member of Joe Scott Post, No. 100, at Zair Lake, Manistee County, Department of Michigan, Grand Army of the Republic.

These facts are thus recorded and preserved for the benefit of all those who may be interested.

o-oo-oo-oo-oo-oo-oo-oo-oo-o

Harry Fay Woodbury
1897 - 1981

Harry Woodbury was born on September 12,1897 in Lennawee County, Michigan to
John Milton and Anna Woodbury. Harry served in the National Guard during WW1.
He married Alice Bosenbark on September 2, 1920. He worked for the Fire Department
and owned Woodbury's Bar in Monroe, Michigan. Harry passed away on December
23,1981. Harry was was the father of three sons . Alice passed away in1994 He is now
survived by his son Raymond Woodbury , grand children and gr-grandchildren.

SGT. Harry Woodbury
Woodbury

2nd Lt. Harry

Harry was in the Michigan National Guard in
WW1. His unit from Monroe Mi. was eventually
called to active duty. They were on board ship
when the war ended, so it turned around before it
reached the 12 mile limit. After the war he stayed
in the guard until around 1930.The guard used to
train in Grayling Michigan in the fall of the year,
and before he left each year him and Alice would
start a batch of home made beer for when he came
home. It was during prohibition and you had to
make your own. When he came home from
training he would always bring home with him
Charlie and Brice Custer. They were Great Grand
nephews of General Custer and served in the guard
with Harry.

Louis Shanaway Jr.
1888-1924

Louis Shanaway was born on April 15,1888 in Illinois to Louis and Mary Kane
Shanaway. Louis enlisted in the Army during World War I. Loius was wounded and he
died of his wounds January of 1924. He was married to Maude Woodbury and they had
three children. His daughter Mary Shanaway Wagner still survives him and lives in New
Port, Michigan. She will be 84 and is the Senior Woodbury Family member.

Jessie Shanaway
1924-1946

Jessie was born on January 9,1924 to Louis and Maude (Woodbury) Shanaway.
He was born in the same month as his father died.
During World War II, Jessie enlisted in the Air Force, and on January 15,1946 he was
listed as missing in action and presumed dead in the Pacific Ocean.

Milton Osenbaugh

Milton Osenbaugh the son of Iva (Woodbury) and Zenith Osenbaugh. Milton served in
WWII from January 3,1945 until he was discharged at the end of the war on July 3,
1946. Milton served on the U.S.S. FALL RIVER stationed at Newport, R.1..
   On January 1, 1952 he married his wife Mary and they resided in New York. Milton
and Mary had five daughters, Shelia ,Debbie,Kathy,Janet, and Jackie. Milton is now
retired and lives in Zypherhills, Fla,

Louis Leander Shanaway
1920-1982

Louie was born on July1, 1920 in Monroe ,Michigan to Lious and Maude (Woodbury) Shanaway . He married Barbara Steward on August 15,1941 in Toledo,Ohio. During WWII Louis joined the U.S. Army and fought in the South Pacific. Louie moved his family to LaBelle, Florida in the late fifties, then to Central Florida in the 70's. Louie was the father of seven children, Jeannie, David , Mike, Karen, Dennis, Marvin and Leanne. Barb died January 15,1982, and Louie on December 7,1982 .

John Woodbury
1911-1992

Johnny Woodbury was born to Herman and Emma (Shanaway) Woodbury in Monroe, Michigan in 1911. He married Corrine Monroe. They had six children. Johnny entered the U.S. Army in 1943 during World War II . After the war he worked as a laborer and lived in Swanton. Ohio. In 1954 he moved with his family to Cocoa, Florida where they remained until his death on January 15, 1992.His wife Corrine died 1995 He is survived by sons Jack of California, Ron of North Carolina,and Jim of Florida.

Zenith (Babe) Osenbaugh
1925-1999

Babe was born on May 26,1925 to Zenith and Iva (Woodbury) Osenbaugh.
He served in the U.S.Army in World War II in the Pacific. He married Dorthy Haekos
and had seven children. He then married Vivian (Bunker)in 1972. Babe worked for
American Ship Builders for many years , until an industrial accident disabled him .Babe
had done many things from a dealer in Las Vegas to running a gas station in Florida. He
was a jack of all trades Babe died June 7, 1999.and is burried in Restlawn cemetary in
Perrysburg, Ohio. He is survived by his wife Vivian his children and many grandchildren.

John Spangler

John was born December 22,1925, to Helen (Rahm- Conlin)Spangler & John Conlin.
On December 22,1952   John married Marge Baker Sutton. John enlisted in the
U.S.Army Air Force in 1943. He served in the European Theater and was at Omaha
Beach invasion. After the war John came home and worked at the Champion Spark Plug
factory, worked Eddie Rahm ,doing television repairs , and was a truck driver for many
years. John is now retired and he and Marge live in Toledo, Oh

Ralph Woodbury
1928- 1986

Ralph William Woodbury was born October 8,1928 in Monroe, Michigan to Harry and
Alice Woodbury. On Janurary 30,1955 he married Donna Sype. Ralph served in the
Second Armored Division , in Germany., from 1950 until 1952. . He passed away on
April16, 1986. he is survived by his wife and children Loretta and Ralph Jr.

Herbert Slater
1928- 1981

Herb was born on August26,1928. He was the husband of Beverly Osenbaugh. He
served as a PFC3 in the U.S. Army in Germany from 1951-1953.Herb passed away from
Cancer on February 15,1981. Beverly passed away in 1994. They are buried in Restlawn
Cemetary in Perrysburg, Ohio. They are survived by their son Charles in Alpena,
Michigan.

William Woodbury
1936- 1996

Bill was born to Johnny and Corrine(Monroe) Woodbury on March 29,1936. He attended scool in the Swanton, Ohio schools. Bill joined the Marine Corps in the early fifties. He married Violet Cabb on October 13,1956. He was the father of five children, and lived in North Carolina. Bill died of Cancer in 1996, and Vi of cancer in 1997. they are survived by their children , Dorthy Strong, William , Darlene, Connie , Brenda.

Edward Sonny Rahm
1938-1997

Sonny was born February 2, 1938 to Edward and Nola (Woodbury)Rahm.He
enlisted in the U.S. Air Force in 1953, and did his basic traning in Sampson, New York
then on to Cheyanne,Wyoming then overseas to Japan and Korea. Sonny was discharged
in 1956 on a hardship to come home and help his parents in their television repair
bussiness. Sonny married Patrica Kothe in 1958 and they had 2 children. He married
Marlene Jewel on December 31,1991 and they lived in Holland Ohio. Sonny worked for
Hunt Wesseon Foods as an electrician. Sonny died from lung cancer on August 4,1997.
Sonnys hobby was restoring old cars. He won a National Championship Trophy for his
1954 Lincoln (SWEET THING) in January 1997.

David Shanaway
1947- 1996

David Shanaway was born on May 10, 1947 in Toledo, oh To Louis and Barbra
Shanaway. He married Jennie Watkins on April 28,1969 . David served in the Navy
during the Vietnam War. He moved to Central Florida in1979.David worked as a driller
for Ardaman & Assoc.in Orlando, Florida . He was a Scout master for the Boy Scouts
and a trustee for the Kirkman Road United Methodist Church.
David died January 9, 1995 of a massive Stroke . He is survived by his wife Belinda and
sons Brian & Elvan Norman ,daughter Victoria Leigh-Norman all of Orlando, Fl.

Larry Dean Beaty
1945-1968

Larry was born to Richard (Red)and Dorthy(Houck) Beaty on December 18,1945 in
Toledo,Ohio.Larry joined the U.S. Army in and served a tour of duty in Vietnam. he
returned to Toledo in and was murdered on March 4,1968. Larry is buried at Toledo
Memorial Cemetary , in Sylvania, Ohio.

Others who served

Jim Kurtz.......U.S.Army, Jim is the husband of Sue (Hinds) Kurtz
Jim and Sue live in Naples, and have a daughter Jami.

Jim Woodbury........Jim is the son of Johnny & Corrine Woodbury. Jim
was born in Toledo ,Oh on July 14,1947. he married Ruth Goethe on May
28, 1966. Jim is retired from the service and he is the father of four
children, and lives in Rockledge, Florida.

Rafael Velasquez.....U.S. Navy...Retired ... Ralph is the husband of LuAnn
(Woodbury) He was born in the Phillipines. He and Luann were married
on July3.1961. Luann passed away in January of this year. Ralph lives in
Cocoa, Florida. They had five children . Terry, Vivian, Grego, Alex, and
Angela.

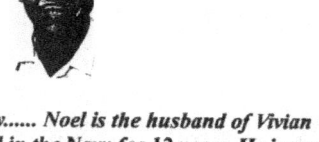

Noel Remillard...U.S. Navy...... Noel is the husband of Vivian
(Shrewsbury). Noel served in the Navy for 12 years. He is now a Deputy
with the Brevard County Sheriffs Office. Noel and Viv live in Cocoa,
Florida

Gary Musser... was born to Dale and Edith (Woodbury)Musser on July 9,
1957. Gary served in the U.S. Army. He and his wife Donna live in
Middleburg , Florida and has six children.

Larry Musser...was born to Dale and Edith (Woodbury)Musser on July
9,1957. Larry served in the U.S. Marines. Larry and his wife live in
Sylvania, Oh and have five children.

Others who served

Terry Woodbury... Terry was born to Luann Woodbury on January 6,1958 in Cocoa, Florida. Terry served in the U.S. Navy. Terry and his wifr Michelle live in Fort Walton Beach, Florida. Terry is a fireman with the Ft. Walton Beach Fire Department. Terry has six children.

Cecil Woodbury Jr. Cecil was born to Cecil and Idabelle (Long) Woodbury in Toledo Ohio. He served in the U.S. Navy in the mid fifties. He is married to Delores Duty and the have two children , Don & Sherry. Cecil owns a silk flower shop in Toledo.

Jack Woodbury Served in the early fifties, and is married to Norma and lives in California.

John Snyder was born to Iva (Woodbury) & Art Snyder on March 20, 1946John served in the U.S. Army. He is married to Virginia , and they live in Wachula , FL. John is the father of five children.

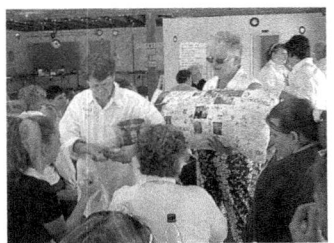 

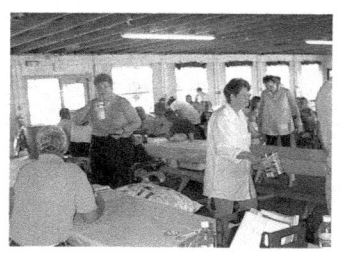

Woodbury

Reunion

2005

Woodbury

Reunion

2006

Woodbury

Reunion

2007

Woodbury

Reunion

2017

How the 2017 Reunion got started!!

Richard Hinds
July 10, 2016

We need to have a Hinds family reunion

👍 Like 💬 Comment

 Wanda Allen, Debbie Hinds and 11 others ✓ Seen by 79

Darlene Hinds Yes we really need too
Like · Reply · July 10, 2016 at 6:29pm

Donald Mannon Agree
Like · Reply · ⊙ 1 · July 10, 2016 at 6:31pm

Debbie Hinds Agreed
Like · Reply · ⊙ 1 · July 10, 2016 at 6:55pm

Terrie Perry Agree
Like · Reply · ⊙ 1 · July 10, 2016 at 7:40pm

Evelyn Johnson I agree
Like · Reply · ⊙ 1 · July 10, 2016 at 7:42pm

Donald Mannon Road trip lol
Like · Reply · ⊙ 2 · July 10, 2016 at 7:43pm

Mary Hinds Yes for sure.. I'm in
Like · Reply · ⊙ 1 · July 10, 2016 at 7:52pm

Sherry Hinds Im in I would love to see everyone
Like · Reply · ⊙ 1 · July 10, 2016 at 9:47pm

Marjorie Hinds Scott Agreed
Like · Reply · ⊙ 1 · July 10, 2016 at 10:59pm

Donald Mannon I'm ready for a vacation. All I do is work lol
Like · Reply · ⊙ 2 · July 10, 2016 at 11:01pm

Marjorie Hinds Scott Well let's do it. I'd like to meet more of our family and
reunite with those I haven't seen in years!
Who wants to be in charge????
Like · Reply · ⊙ 1 · July 10, 2016 at 11:05pm

> **Mary Hinds** I vote you Marjorie Hinds Scott lol
> Like · Reply · July 11, 2016 at 1:31pm
>
> Write a reply 📷 ☺

Marie Hinds I'm all in but we better just get a very very large place because
there are a lot of us!
Like · Reply · ⊙ 1 · July 11, 2016 at 1:13pm

Reunion Location

The facility for the reunion is the Tom Bevill Enrichment Center. It is located at 115 Main Street in Rainsville, Alabama. We will have the whole building from 9:00 am to 9:00 pm on Saturday, March 11, 2017. It has an auditorium, kitchen, outdoor playground, volleyball area and basketball courts.

The reunion hours will be from 10:00 am to 7:30 pm in order to allow for setup and cleanup.

Tables and chairs are included in the rental. The kitchen is equipped with a stove, oven, refrigerator, dishwasher and microwave.

From their website - "The building's auditorium features a cathedral ceiling and a hardwood floor. With a comfortable seating capacity of up to about 280, the auditorium also features a stage and a PA system. Over 200 chairs and a variety of tables are available for use at no extra charge."

Richard Hinds / Hinds Heating & Cooling has paid the deposit and is planning on footing the entire bill, which is $375.00. I told Rich that we would collect the money to pay him back and he said no. He wants us to use the money we do collect to pay for food and other expenses related to the reunion.

Reunion Location

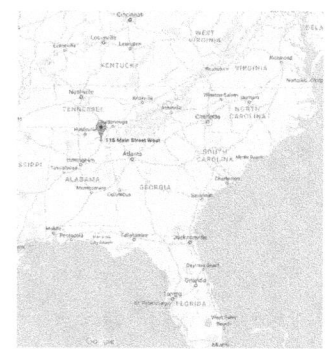

Descendants of John Wellington Hinds

First Generation

1. **John Wellington Hinds** was born on 7 Feb 1772 in Cayuga, NY. He died on 25 May 1812. He was buried in East Liverpool, Columbiana County, Ohio, USA.

   John married **Cynthia Olive White** daughter of Isaac White and Priscilla Moffatt about 1794. Cynthia was born on 27 Jul 1773 in Adams, Berkshire, Massachusetts, USA. She died on 10 Aug 1855 in Dresden, Muskingum, Ohio, USA.

   They had the following children:

	2 M	i.	**Richard Hinds** was born on 21 May 1809. He died on 1 Jan 1813.
	3 M	ii.	**Lyman Hinds** was born on 16 Aug 1807.
+	4 M	iii.	**Alfred White HINDS reelected Justice of the Peace elected Justice of the Peace** was born on 11 May 1811. He died on 17 Apr 1875.
	5 M	iv.	**Simon Hinds** was born on 16 Aug 1807.
	6 F	v.	**Sally Hinds** was born on 10 Sep 1798.
	7 F	vi.	**Amercy Hinds** was born on 4 Sep 1805.
	8 F	vii.	**Sarah Hinds** was born on 13 Sep 1796.
	9 M	viii.	**Isaac White Hinds** was born on 24 Feb 1795.
	10 M	ix.	**John W Hinds** was born on 4 May 1798. He died on 27 Feb 1876. He was buried in Lexington, Scott County, Indiana, USA. John married **Catherine** . Catherine was born in 1796. She died on 6 Nov 1870. She was buried in Lexington, Scott County, Indiana, USA.
	11 F	x.	**Alphratus Hinds** was born on 10 Nov 1803 in Georgetown, Beaver, Pennsylvania, USA. She died on 16 Feb 1813 in Whiteford, Monroe, Michigan, USA.
+	12 M	xi.	**Almon White Hinds** was born on 13 Sep 1800.

Second Generation

4. Alfred White HINDS reelected Justice of the Peace elected Justice of the Peace (John Wellington) was born on 11 May 1811 in Georgetown, Beaver, Pennsylvania, USA. He died on 17 Apr 1875 in Whiteford, Monroe, Michigan, USA.

Alfred married **Sarah A Shilling** daughter of Robert Shilling and Sarah Newport on 30 Oct 1831 in Dresden, Muskingum, Ohio, USA. Sarah was born on 19 Sep 1812 in Kent, England. She died on 17 Aug 1879 in Whiteford, Monroe, Michigan, USA. She was buried on 18 Aug 1879 in Sylvania, Lucas, Ohio, USA.

They had the following children:

	13 F	i.	**Laura Frances Hinds** was born on 7 May 1850 in Ohio, USA. She died on 10 May 1856.
	14 M	ii.	**William Theadore Hinds** was born on 29 Apr 1847 in Ohio, USA. He died on 6 Oct 1850.
+	15 M	iii.	**Alfred Edward Hinds** was born on 6 Dec 1844. He died on 24 Dec 1899.
	16 F	iv.	**Laura Frances HINDS** was born on 7 May 1850. She died on 10 May 1856.
+	17 M	v.	**Harvey Wilson Hinds** was born on 18 Aug 1854.
+	18 M	vi.	**George Almond Hinds** was born on 24 Mar 1852.
+	19 M	vii.	**Lyman Robert Hinds** was born on 17 Jan 1836. He died on 19 Jul 1921.
	20 F	viii.	**Cynthia Phebe Hinds** was born on 22 Oct 1833 in Michigan, USA. She died on 26 Sep 1902 in Sturgis, St Joseph, Michigan. Cynthia married (1) **Oliver CHARLES Potter** on 30 Nov 1853 in Whiteford, Monroe, Michigan, USA. Oliver was born on 2 Oct 1826 in Madison, New York. He died on 24 Dec 1864. Cynthia married (2) **George W Short** on 24 Jan 1865 in Putnam Co. George was born about 1831. He died in 1865.
	21 M	ix.	**John R. Hinds** was born on 24 Oct 1832. He died on 24 Oct 1832.
+	22 F	x.	**Sarah Louisa Hinds** was born on 11 Dec 1842. She died on 30 Apr 1926.
	23 M	xi.	**Francis Asbury Hinds** was born on 4 Mar 1840. He died on 30 Sep 1845.
	24 M	xii.	**Thomas Josiah Hinds** was born on 14 Apr 1839 in Whiteford, Monroe, Michigan, USA. He died on 27 Apr 1865 in Steamer

Sultana, Held Memphis, Tennessee, USA. He was buried in Memphis, Shelby, Tennessee, USA.

12. **Almon White Hinds** (John Wellington) was born on 13 Sep 1800.

Almon married **Margaret McGregor** daughter of Matthew McGregor and Mary Walker.

Margaret was born in 1792.

They had the following children:

+   25 M   i.   **John Hinds** was born on 22 May 1828. He died about 1892.

Third Generation

15. **Alfred Edward Hinds** (Alfred White HINDS, John Wellington) was born on 6 Dec 1844 in Dresden, Muskingum, Ohio, USA. He died on 24 Dec 1899 in Whiteford, MI, Toledo, Ohio, USA. He was buried in Willow Cemetery, Lucas County, Ohio.

Alfred married **Emily May Rice** daughter of Rodney Stephen Rice and Rowena R. Fuller on 12 Jul 1898 in Toledo, Lucas, Ohio, USA. Emily was born on 22 Jan 1860 in Toledo, Lucas, Ohio. She died on 24 Mar 1958 in Toledo, Lucas, Ohio.

They had the following children:

    26 F   i.   **Edna May Hinds** was born on 26 Jun 1882 in Michigan.

    27 F   ii.   **Ruby Perl Hinds** was born on 1 Jun 1885 in Michigan. She died on 15 Nov 1889 in Toledo city, Lucas, Ohio.

    28 F   iii.   **Ada Leola Hinds** was born on 29 May 1876 in Ottowa Lake, Monroe, MI. She died on 15 Apr 1979 in California.

    29 M   iv.   **Edward Murl Hinds** was born on 28 Feb 1878 in Monroe County, Michigan. He died on 8 Aug 1972 in Toledo, Lucas, Ohio. Edward married **Ella Roe** on 12 Jul 1898. Ella was born in 1879.

17. **Harvey Wilson Hinds** (Alfred White HINDS, John Wellington) was born on 18 Aug 1854 in Michigan.

Harvey married **Jessie May Hartley** daughter of Daniel Beaton Hartley and Mary E Thorn on 6 Oct 1886 in Henry County, Ohio. Jessie was born in 1870 in , , Ohio, USA. She died on 24 Feb 1915 in York Twp., Fulton County, Ohio.

They had the following children:

+   30 M   i.   **Hartley White Hinds** was born on 19 Mar 1888. He died on 8 Mar 1971.

18. **George Almond Hinds** (Alfred White HINDS, John Wellington) was born on 24 Mar 1852 in Ohio, USA. He died in Whiteford, Monroe, Michigan, USA.

George married **Emma Clara Thornburgh** in 1876. Emma was born on 22 Apr 1853. She died on 20 Oct 1933.

They had the following children:

    31 M   i. **Harry F Hinds** was born in Apr 1884 in Ohio.

    32 F   ii. **Ethel C Hinds** was born in Oct 1880 in Michigan.

    33 F   iii. **Louise L Hinds** was born in Jul 1887 in Ohio.

    34 F   iv. **Robert Laker Hinds** was born on 13 Aug 1878 in Ottawa Lake, Monroe,

        Michigan.

    35 F   v. **Mabel L Hinds** was born in Sep 1892 in Ohio.

19. **Lyman Robert Hinds** (Alfred White HINDS, John Wellington) was born on 17 Jan 1836 in Huron, Erie, Ohio, USA. He died on 19 Jul 1921 in Homeland Ga--Buried in Sylvania , Ohio. He was buried in Sylvania, Lucas, Ohio, USA.

Lyman married (1) **Phoebe Augusta Hopkins** on 15 Sep 1861 in Whiteford, Monroe, Michigan, USA. Phoebe was born on 17 Dec 1842 in Dundee, New York. She died on 12 Jul 1902 in Whiteford, Monroe, Michigan, USA. She was buried in Sylvania, Lucas, Ohio, USA.

They had the following children:

    36 F   i. **Winfred Hinds** was born on 30 Mar 1881.

    37 M   ii. **Frankie Hinds** was born on 19 Oct 1879. He died on 27 Oct 1879.

+   38 F   iii. **Sarah Elizabeth Sadie Hinds** was born on 11 Feb 1876. She died on 5 Jun 1958.

    39 F   iv. **Maud Hinds** was born about 1883 in Pennsylvania.

    40 F   v. **Clara Hinds** was born on 15 Mar 1888 in Michigan, USA. She died on 5 Aug 1888 in Whiteford, Monroe, Michigan, USA.

+   41 M   vi. **Mark Aaron Hinds** was born on 28 Jul 1883. He died on 10 Oct 1951.

+   42 M   vii. **John White Hinds** was born on 12 Dec 1873. He died in 1946.

+   43 M   viii. **Alfred White Hinds** was born on 13 Feb 1864. He died on 22 Oct 1938.

+ 44 F   ix. **Cynthia Augusta Hinds** was born on 8 Apr 1862. She died on 22 May 1904.

45 F   x. **Roxanna Hinds** .

46 F   xi. **Lettie M Hinds** was born on 26 Oct 1871.

47 M   xii. **Oliver G Hinds** was born on 27 Oct 1869. He died on 12 Apr 1938 in Adrian, Lenawee, Michigan, USA.

+ 48 F   xiii. **Laura L Hinds** was born on 16 May 1866. She died after 1886.

Lyman married (2) **Sarah A. Hinds** . Sarah was born about 1843 in New York.

22. **Sarah Louisa Hinds** (Alfred White HINDS, John Wellington) was born on 11 Dec 1842 in Sylvania, Lucas, Ohio, USA. She died on 30 Apr 1926 in Toledo, Lucas County, Ohio, USA. She was buried in Sylvania, Lucas County, Ohio, USA.

Sarah married **Lester Bradner Decker** son of Jacob C Decker and Almira Decker on 30

Oct 1872 in Whiteford, Monroe, Michigan, USA. Lester was born on 14 Jan 1842 in DANVILLE, (LIVINGSTON) NEW YORK. He died on 26 Feb 1927 in Richfield Center, Lucas County, Ohio, USA. He was buried in Sylvania, Lucas County, Ohio, USA.

They had the following children:

49   i. **Rev Shirley H Decker** was born on 18 Mar 1883 in Sylvania, Lucas County, Ohio, USA. Rev died on 18 Apr 1914 in Sylvania, Lucas County, Ohio, USA. Rev was buried in Sylvania, Lucas County, Ohio, USA.

50   ii. **Harvey C Decker** was born on 5 Jan 1878 in Toledo, Lucas County, Ohio, USA. Harvey died on 26 Jan 1942 in Toledo, Lucas County, Ohio, USA. Harvey was buried in Toledo, Lucas County, Ohio, USA.

+ 51 M   iii. **Vernon Lester Decker** was born on 28 Jul 1881. He died on 16 Jul 1934.

52   iv. **Leroy Decker** was born on 3 Dec 1875. Leroy died on 11 Apr 1886. Leroy was buried in Sylvania, Lucas County, Ohio, USA.

+ 53 F   v. **Florence Ivadell Decker** was born on 18 Mar 1883. She died on 19 Aug 1964.

54   vi. **Park Werter Decker** was born on 22 Aug 1879 in Sylvania, Lucas County, Ohio, USA. Park died in 1957 in Ohio, USA. Park was

buried in Elmore, Ottawa County, Ohio, USA.

<table>
<tr><td>55</td><td>vii.</td><td>Ernest F Decker was born on 14 Apr 1874. Ernest died on 10 May 1874. Ernest was buried in Sylvania, Lucas County, Ohio, USA.</td></tr>
</table>

25. **John Hinds** (Almon White, John Wellington) was born on 22 May 1828 in Robinson Township, Allegheny County, PA, USA. He died about 1892 in , , Pennsylvania, USA.

John married **Rebecca Gano McCague** on 7 Nov 1853 in Allegheny, Allegheny, Pennsylvania, United States. Rebecca was born on 7 Jul 1834 in Manchester, Allegheny County, Pennsylvania. She died in 1905. She was buried in Pittsburgh, Allegheny County, Pennsylvania, USA.

They had the following children:

+   56 M   i.   **William McCague Hinds** was born on 20 Nov 1854. He died on 13 Sep 1942.

+   57 F   ii.   **Margaret Ella Grubbs** was born on 30 Jun 1860. She died on 3 Apr 1942.

      58 M   iii.   **Harry Milton Hinds** was born on 8 Nov 1868 in Beaver, Beaver County, Pennsylvania USA. He died on 14 Aug 1905.

      59 F   iv.   **Emma Ann Hinds** was born on 14 Feb 1858 in Allegheny, Allegheny, Pennsylvania, United States. She died on 16 Aug 1889 in Allegheny, Allegheny, Pennsylvania, United States.

      60 M   v.   **Walter Byron Hinds** was born on 21 Apr 1880 in Beaver, Beaver County, Pennsylvania USA. He died in 1901 in Penslvania, USA.

      61 F   vi.   **Bertha Georgetta Hinds** was born on 1 Nov 1876 in Beaver, Beaver County, Pennsylvania USA.

      62 M   vii.   **Alman Walker Hinds** was born on 21 May 1856 in Allegheny, Allegheny, Pennsylvania, United States. He died on 26 Aug 1869 in Beaver, Beaver County, Pennsylvania, USA.

+   63 M   viii.   **John Grant Hinds** was born in Apr 1865.

      64 M   ix.   **William M Hinds** was born about 1855. He died on 11 Jan 1883 in Allegheny City, Pa.

      65 M   x.   **Walter C Hinds** was born about 1879.

+   66 M   xi.   **Frank French Hinds** was born on 31 Oct 1870.

+   67 F   xii.   **Ida Rebecca Hinds** was born on 17 Sep 1865. She died on 27 Nov 1891.

+ 68 M xiii. **James Elmer Hinds** was born on 21 May 1874. He died on 23 Jan 1936.

69 M xiv. **Charles Elrod Hinds** was born on 12 Jul 1884 in Beaver, Beaver County, Pennsylvania USA. He died on 27 May 1916 in Pittsburgh, Allegheny, Pennsylvania, USA.

Fourth Generation

30. **Hartley White Hinds** (Harvey Wilson Hinds, Alfred White HINDS, John Wellington) was born on 19 Mar 1888 in Toledo, Lucas, Ohio, USA. He died on 8 Mar 1971 in Springfield, Calhoun, Michigan. He was buried in Banfield, Barry County, Michigan, USA.

Hartley married **Florence Jessie Long** daughter of Robert Asher Long and Harriett Emma Laning on 10 Oct 1906 in Lucas County, Ohio, USA. Florence was born on 19 Nov 1888 in Forest, Ohio. She died on 27 May 1983 in Battle Creek, Calhoun, Michigan, USA. She was buried in Banfield, Barry County, Michigan, USA.

They had the following children:

+ 70 F i. **Mildred Isabel Hinds** was born on 3 Jan 1912. She died on 14 Nov 1981.

+ 71 F ii. **Hazel May HINDS** was born on 3 Nov 1909.

+ 72 M iii. **Warren Edmund Hinds** was born on 25 Apr 1923. He died on 7 Nov 1995.

+ 73 M iv. **Hartley Wilbur Hinds** was born on 24 Feb 1916. He died on 20 May 1985.

74 F v. **Wilma Jean Hinds**
Wilma married (1) **Arthur Haas**
Wilma married (2) **Charles Minor**

+ 75 M vi. **Roland Leroy Hinds** was born on 20 Jun 1919. He died on 24 Jun 1961.

+ 76 M vii. **Elroy Bud Hinds** was born on 30 Apr 1907. He died on 3 Nov 1961.

+ 77 F viii. **Bonnie Hinds**

38. **Sarah Elizabeth Sadie Hinds** (Lyman Robert Hinds, Alfred White HINDS, John Wellington) was born on 11 Feb 1876 in Monroe, Michigan, USA. She died on 5 Jun 1958 in Wood Co, OH,. She was buried in at Head O Lake, Ottowa Lake, MI.

Sarah married **Clarence Adelbert Tubbs** on 1 Jun 1897. Clarence was born on 17 Oct 1865 in Whiteford, Monroe, Michigan, United States. He died on 26 Nov 1953 in Wood, Ohio, United States. He was buried in Monroe County, Michigan, USA.

They had the following children:

> 78 M   i.   **Orris Franklin Tubbs** was born on 4 Mar 1899 in Michigan. He died on 11 Nov 1983 in Blissfield, Lenawee, Michigan, United States of America.

> +   79 F   ii.   **Kathryn Augusta Tubbs** was born on 5 Jun 1913. She died on 6 Dec 1977.

> 80 F   iii.   **Clara Sylvia Tubbs** was born on 2 Mar 1901 in Whiteford Monroe Co, Mi. She died on 12 Jan 1962 in Walbridge, Oh Bu: Head Lake Cem OttawaLake.

> 81 M   iv.   **Earl Adelbert Tubbs** was born on 10 Nov 1910 in Whiteford MI (Monroe CO). He died on 24 Sep 1990 in Deerfield, MI.

> 82 F   v.   **Donna Mae Tubbs** was born on 26 Apr 1918 in Michigan. She died on 28 May 2002 in RisingSun, OH Bur Bradner Cem..

41. **Mark Aaron Hinds** (Lyman Robert Hinds, Alfred White HINDS, John Wellington) was born on 28 Jul 1883 in Ottowa Lake, Michigan. He died on 10 Oct 1951 in Duval, Florida, United States. He was buried in Hilliard, Nassau County, Florida, USA.

Mark married **Elizabeth Orra "Lizzie" Williams** after 1905. Elizabeth was born on 22 Jan 1888 in Michigan. She died on 12 May 1969 in Duval, Florida, United States. She was buried in Hilliard, Nassau County, Florida, USA.

They had the following children:

> 83 M   i.   **Aaron R. Hinds** was born on 27 Oct 1913. He died on 29 Oct 1913.

> 84 M   ii.   **Herbert Hinds** was born on 3 Nov 1924. He died on 5 Nov 1924.

42. **John White Hinds** (Lyman Robert Hinds, Alfred White HINDS, John Wellington) was born on 12 Dec 1873. He died in 1946.

John married **Mary Leona Mate Tubbs** about 1900. Mary was born about 1875.

They had the following children:

> 85 F   i.   **Louella Florence Hinds** was born about 1905. She died in 1913.

> 86 M   ii.   **Lyman Hinds** was born about 1907.

+ 87 M   iii. **Lester Earl Hinds** was born about 1901. He died in 1965.

88 F   iv. **Erma Lucille Hinds** was born on 3 May 1903. She died on 11 Jun 1998.
Erma married **George Edgar Burnsed** about 1920. George was born in 1898. He died in 1967.

43. **Alfred White Hinds** (Lyman Robert Hinds, Alfred White HINDS, John Wellington) was born on 13 Feb 1864. He died on 22 Oct 1938. He was buried in Hilliard, Nassau County, Florida, USA.

Alfred married **Roxa Lucinda FOX** on 6 May 1891. Roxa was born on 6 Nov 1868. She died on 14 Oct 1946. She was buried in Hilliard, Nassau County, Florida, USA.

They had the following children:

89   i. **Thelma Grace Eland** was born on 15 Jun 1899 in Michigan, USA. Thelma died on 15 Jun 1989 in Pittsboro, Chatham County, North Carolina, USA. Thelma was buried in Jacksonville, Duval County, Florida, USA.

44. **Cynthia Augusta Hinds** (Lyman Robert Hinds, Alfred White HINDS, John Wellington) was
born on 8 Apr 1862 in Ottawa Lake, Putnam Co, OH. She died on 22 May 1904 in Petersburg, Monroe, Michigan, USA. She was buried in Petersburg, Monroe County, Michigan, USA.

Cynthia married **Willis Walter Heimer** on 15 Apr 1882 in Sylvania, Wood Co, OH. Willis was born on 6 Jul 1858 in Jackson, Susquehanna, Pennsylvania, USA. He died on 17 Aug 1902 in Petersburg, Monroe, Michigan, USA. He was buried in Pleasantview Cem, Summerfield Twp, MI.

They had the following children:

90 F   i. **Laura Maude Heimer** was born on 25 Mar 1883 in Thompson, Susquehanna, Pennsylvania, United States. She died in of Oneata, New York, USA.

91 M   ii. **Arlington S. Heimer** was born on 8 Mar 1882 in Sylvania, Wood, Ohio, United States. He died on 10 Feb 1889 in Sylvania, Wood, Ohio, United States.

92 M   iii. **Albert Samuel Heimer** was born on 28 Nov 1894 in Ararat, Susquehanna, Pennsylvania, USA. He died on 11 Aug 1982 in Vallejo, Solano, California, United States. He was buried in Petersburg, Monroe County, Michigan.

93 F   iv. **Iva Himer** was born on 13 Apr 1900 in Petersburg, Monroe, Michigan, United States. She died on 9 Sep 1901 in Petersburg, Monroe, Michigan, United States.

94 F   v.   **Celia Valara Severia Heimer** was born on 26 Mar 1898 in Petersburg, Monroe, Michigan, United States. She died on 16 May 1977 in Franklin, Essex, New Jersey, USA. She was buried in Hamburg, Sussex County, New Jersey.

95 M   vi.   **Iva Heimer** was born on 13 Apr 1900 in Petersburg, Monroe, Colorado, United States. He died on 9 Sep 1901 in Petersburg, Monroe, Michigan, United States.

96 F   vii.   **Oma May Heimer** was born on 12 May 1896 in Summerfield, Monroe, Michigan, United States. She died in 1924.

97 F   viii.   **Emma Pearl Heimer** was born on 17 Mar 1892 in Ararat, Susquehanna, Pennsylvania, USA. She died on 8 May 1976 in St Lukes Hospital in Maumee, Wood, Ohio, USA.

98 F   ix.   **Inis Alpharetta Heimer** was born on 18 Feb 1886 in Ararat, Susquehanna, Pennsylvania, USA. She died on 4 Jul 1973 in Toledo, Lucas, Ohio, USA.

99 F   x.   **Oressa Myrtle Heimer** was born on 5 Apr 1890 in Forest City, Susquehanna, Pennsylvania, United States. She died in 1915.

48. **Laura L Hinds** (Lyman Robert Hinds, Alfred White HINDS, John Wellington) was born on 16 May 1866. She died after 1886.

Laura married **Philo Thomas Mills** son of Ransom W Mills and Louisa Maria Bunting about 1886. Philo was born on 13 Jan 1868 in Michigan. He died after 1886.

They had the following children:

100 F   i.   **Gladys L Mills** was born on 31 Jul 1897 in Toledo, Lucas, Ohio.

51. **Vernon Lester Decker** (Sarah Louisa Hinds, Alfred White HINDS, John Wellington) was born on 28 Jul 1881 in Sylvania, Lucas County, Ohio, USA. He died on 16 Jul 1934 in Sylvania, Lucas County, Ohio, USA. He was buried in Toledo, Lucas County, Ohio, USA.

Vernon married **Amy Louise Permar** daughter of William J Permar and Thirza N Permar. Amy was born on 25 Nov 1881 in Pt Clinton, Ottawa, Ohio. She died in 1954. She was buried in Toledo, Lucas County, Ohio, USA.

They had the following children:

101 F   i.   **Naomi Ruth Decker** was born on 3 Feb 1914 in Ohio.

102 F   ii.   **Betty F Decker** was born about 1916 in Ohio.

103 M   iii.   **Lester Decker** was born on 18 Jul 1903 in Lucas County, Ohio,

USA. He died in Nov 1985 in Detroit, Wayne, Michigan, United States.

+   104 F   iv. **Myra Louise Decker** was born on 27 Dec 1909. She died on 2 Aug 1971.

53. **Florence Ivadell Decker** (Sarah Louisa Hinds, Alfred White HINDS, John Wellington) was born on 18 Mar 1883 in Sylvania, Lucas County, Ohio, USA. She died on 19 Aug 1964 in Sylvania, Ohio, USA. She was buried in Sylvania, Lucas County, Ohio, USA.

Florence married **Arthur Burton Sloan** on 9 Jun 1909. Arthur was born on 24 Jan 1876 in Richfield, Lucas, Ohio, USA. He died on 29 Sep 1937 in Sylvania, Lucas, Ohio, USA.

They had the following children:

   105 M   i. **Richard Hall Sloan** was born on 6 Jul 1913 in Ohio. He died on 20 Jul 1985 in Toledo, Lucas, Ohio.

   106 M   ii. **Robert Shilling Sloan** was born on 6 Jul 1913 in Ohio. He died on 8 Sep 1972. He was buried in Fulton County, Ohio, USA.

   107 M   iii. **LeRoy Arthur Sloan** was born on 19 Jun 1910 in Ohio. He died on 3 Sep 1998.

+   108 F   iv. **Florence Louisa Sloan** was born on 3 Apr 1920. She died on 7 Nov 1994.

   109 M   v. **William Bradner Sloan** was born on 9 Dec 1927 in Ohio. He died on 31 Dec 1999.

   110 M   vi. **Shirley Horatio Sloan** was born on 8 Apr 1916 in Henry, Ohio, United States. He died on 29 Nov 1999 in Sylvania, Lucas, Ohio. He was buried in OH.

56. **William McCague Hinds** (John, Almon White, John Wellington) was born on 20 Nov 1854 in Pittsburgh, Allegheny County, PA, USA. He died on 13 Sep 1942 in Pittsburgh, Allegheny County, PA, USA.

William married **Minnie Thompson** on 28 Nov 1883 in Allegheny, Allegheny, Pennsylvania, United States. Minnie was born on 13 May 1860 in Washington County, PA, USA. She died on 4 Oct 1927 in Pittsburgh, Allegheny County, Pennsylvania, USA.

They had the following children:

   111 M   i. **Howard McCague Hinds** was born on 1 Sep 1886 in Allegheny County, PA, USA. He died on 25 Mar 1975 in Meadville, Crawford County, PA, USA. He was buried in Pittsburgh, Allegheny County, Pennsylvania, USA.

112 F   ii. **Beulah Estella Hinds** was born on 14 Feb 1891 in Allegheny, Allegheny, Pennsylvania, United States. She died on 25 Apr 1893 in Allegheny, Allegheny, Pennsylvania, United States.

113 M   iii. **Loyal Blaine Hinds** was born on 31 Oct 1894 in Allegheny, Allegheny, Pennsylvania, United States. He died on 17 Aug 1956 in Pittsburgh, Allegheny, Pennsylvania, USA.

57. **Margaret Ella Grubbs** (John, Almon White, John Wellington) was born on 30 Jun 1860 in Allegheny, Allegheny, Pennsylvania, United States. She died on 3 Apr 1942 in Pittsburgh, Allegheny, Pennsylvania, USA.

Margaret married **Thomas Fletcher Grubbs** . Thomas was born in Sep 1867 in Allegheny County, Pennsylvania, USA. He died on 15 Jan 1956 in Pittsburgh, Pa.

They had the following children:

114 M   i. **Paul C Grubbs** was born on 6 Feb 1898 in Pittsburgh, Allegheny, Pennsylvania, USA. He died on 27 Apr 1990 in Saegertown, Crawford, Pennsylvania, USA.

115 M   ii. **Luther J Grubbs** was born on 24 Dec 1895 in Mars, Butler Co. Pennsylvania. He died on 18 Sep 1971 in Millvale, Pennsylvania.

116 M   iii. **Percy E B Grubbs** was born about 1906 in Pennsylvania. He died in Nov 1983.

117 M   iv. **Earl Grubbs** was born on 23 May 1906. He died in Nov 1983.

118 M   v. **Edward Dale Grubbs** was born on 6 Nov 1892 in Pittsburgh, Pa. He died in Jun 1981.

119 F   vi. **Ester Brooks** was born in 1904 in Pittsburgh.

120 M   vii. **Westley F Grubbs** was born on 20 Apr 1900 in Pennsylvania. He died in Oct 1979.

121 F   viii. **Estella Grubbs** was born on 19 Nov 1903 in Pittsburgh. She died in Feb 1985.

63. **John Grant Hinds** (John, Almon White, John Wellington) was born in Apr 1865 in Allegheny, Allegheny, Pennsylvania, United States.

John married **Mary J. Gant** on 18 Jun 1889 in Allegheny, Pennsylvania, USA. Mary was born on 26 Apr 1865 in Pittsburgh, Allegheny, Pennsylvania, USA.

They had the following children:

122 M   i. **John G Hinds Jr.** was born in Aug 1890 in Pennsylvania, USA.

123 M   ii. **Charles Newton Hinds** was born on 21 Nov 1892 in Pennsylvania, USA. He died in Pennslyvania, USA.

124 F   iii. **May Hinds** was born in Jan 1898 in Pennsylvania.

125 F   iv. **Loretta Hinds** was born in Jul 1893 in Pennsylvania.

126 M   v. **Lew Hinds** was born in Nov 1896 in Pennsylvania.

66. **Frank French Hinds** (John, Almon White, John Wellington) was born on 31 Oct 1870 in Beaver, Beaver County, Pennsylvania USA.

Frank married **Nelly Parker** on 5 Oct 1897 in Atlantic City, Atlantic, New Jersey, USA. Nelly was born in Dec 1878 in New Jersey.

They had the following children:

127 F   i. **Bertha G Hinds** was born on 10 Feb 1898 in New Jersey. She died in Jul 1972 in Havertown, Delaware, Pennsylvania, United States of America.

128 F   ii. **Elizabeth Hinds** was born about 1897 in New Jersey.

129 F   iii. **Edna Hinds** was born in 1904 in New Jersey.

130 M   iv. **Frank Hinds** was born in 1904 in New Jersey.

67. **Ida Rebecca Hinds** (John, Almon White, John Wellington) was born on 17 Sep 1865 in Beaver, Beaver County, Pennsylvania USA. She died on 27 Nov 1891 in Allegheny, Allegheny, Pennsylvania, United States. She was buried in Pittsburgh, Allegheny County, Pennsylvania.

Ida married **E Calvin Beatty** . E Calvin Beatty was born in Pennsylvania.

E Calvin Beatty and Ida had the following children:

131 F   i. **Barbara Beatty** was born about 1898 in Pennsylvania.

132 M   ii. **Marshall Beatty** was born about 1904 in Pennsylvania.

133 M   iii. **Bruce R Beatty** was born about 1905 in Pennsylvania.

134 F   iv. **Ida Beatty** .

135 M   v. **Elliott B Beatty** was born about 1885 in Pennsylvania.

136 F   vi. **Margarette Beatty** was born about 1896 in Pennsylvania.

68. **James Elmer Hinds** (John, Almon White, John Wellington) was born on 21 May 1874 in Beaver, Beaver County, Pennsylvania USA. He died on 23 Jan 1936 in Pittsburgh, Allegheny, Pennsylvania, USA.

James married (1) **Elizabeth Frankland** in 1913 in Brooke. Elizabeth was born about 1894 in Pennsylvania.

They had the following children:

137 M   i.   **James Hinds** was born about 1915 in Pennsylvania.

138 F   ii.   **Lauretta Hinds** was born about 1918 in Pennsylvania. She died about 1995.

139 M   iii.   **Private** .

140 M   iv.   **Robert Hugh Hinds** was born on 15 Jun 1919 in Pittsburgh, Allegheny, Pennsylvania, USA.

James married (2) **Genevieve Hinds** . Genevieve was born in 1882 in Ohio.

Fifth Generation

70. **Mildred Isabel Hinds** (Hartley White Hinds, Harvey Wilson Hinds, Alfred White HINDS, John Wellington) was born on 3 Jan 1912 in Toledo, Lucas, Ohio, USA. She died on 14 Nov 1981 in Birmingham, Jefferson, Alabama, USA.

Mildred married **John Chesley Robertson** son of John Chealen Robertson and Mattie Rebecca Hallman. John was born on 14 Aug 1906 in Clay County, Alabama, USA. He died on 1 Aug 1980 in Morris, Jefferson, Alabama, USA.

They had the following children:

141 M   i.   **John Hartley Robertson** was born on 25 Oct 1936. He died in May 1968.

142 M   ii.   **Bill Robertson** .

143 F   iii.   **Joan Lee Robertson** was born on 24 Dec 1931 in Ohio, USA. She died on 7 Jun 2008 in Birmingham, Jefferson, Alabama. She was buried in Birmingham, Jefferson County, Alabama, United States of America.

144 F   iv.   **Carol Ann Robertson** was born on 4 Dec 1939 in Birmingham, Jefferson, Alabama, USA. She died on 6 Aug 2006 in Mauldin, Greenville, South Carolina, USA.

145 F   v.   **Jean Robertson**

71. **Hazel May HINDS** (Hartley White Hinds, Harvey Wilson Hinds, Alfred White HINDS, John Wellington) was born on 3 Nov 1909 in Toledo, Lucas, Ohio, USA.

Hazel married **Harry James ROGERS** son of William John ROGERS and Helen Elizabeth Bodinus about 1927. Harry was born on 6 Jul 1898 in Toledo, Lucas County, Ohio, USA. He died on 19 Feb 1989 in Herron, Alpena, Michigan, USA.

They had the following children:

+   146 M   i.   **Harry James Rogers** was born on 25 May 1928. He died on 4 Oct 1977.

72. **Warren Edmund Hinds** (Hartley White Hinds, Harvey Wilson Hinds, Alfred White HINDS, John Wellington) was born on 25 Apr 1923 in New Albany J, Indiana. He died on 7 Nov 1995 in Talladega, Talladega, Alabama, United States of America.

Warren married (1) **Agnes Jeanette Walker** .

They had the following children:

+   147 F   i.   **Beverly Jo Hinds**

+   148 F   ii.   **Jeanette Hinds**

+   149 M   iii.   **Warren Glenn Hinds**

Warren married (2) **Dolores Jean Whalen** on 9 Apr 1988 in Cropwell, Alabama. Dolores was born on 15 Dec 1930. She died on 22 Aug 2010 in Talladega, Talladega, Alabama.

73. **Hartley Wilbur Hinds** (Hartley White Hinds, Harvey Wilson Hinds, Alfred White HINDS, John Wellington) was born on 24 Feb 1916 in Toledo, Lucas, Ohio, USA. He died on 20 May 1985 in Naples, Collier, Florida, USA. He was buried in Cremated.

Hartley married **Laura Louise Woodbury** daughter of John Milton Woodbury and Anna Eliza Cornwill on 22 Jul 1933 in Monroe, Michigan, USA. Laura was born on 19 Aug 1916 in Toledo, Lucas, Ohio, USA. She died on 31 Aug 1989 in Naples, Collier, Florida, USA. She was buried in Cremated.

They had the following children:

+   150 M   i.   **Jimmy Alan Hinds** was born on 26 Feb 1947. He died on 27 Jun 2001.

+   151 M   ii.   **Tommy Gene Hinds** was born on 20 May 1944. He died on 29 May 2005.

+   152 F   iii.   **Kathleen Ann Hinds**

+   153 M   iv.   **Hartley William Hinds**

      154 M   v.   **Keith Ray Hinds** was born on 12 Feb 1952 in Toledo, Lucas, Ohio, USA. He died on 26 Aug 2011 in Naples, Collier, Florida.

Keith married **Recinda Joy Kennison** on 6 Oct 1990 in Collier, Florida.

    155 F   vi.   **Anna Marie Hinds** was born on 15 Sep 1942 in Toledo, Lucas, Ohio, USA. She died on 28 Dec 1943 in Toledo, Lucas, Ohio, United States.

+   156 F   vii.   **Nancy Jean Hinds** was born on 8 May 1936. She died on 28 Mar 1988.

+   157 F   viii.   **Patsy Louise Hinds** was born on 4 Oct 1934. She died on 19 Oct 2006.

+   158 M   ix.   **Jerry Eugene Hinds** was born on 24 Mar 1938. He died on 15 Sep 2005.

+   159 F   x.   **Sandra Sue Hinds**

+   160 M   xi.   **Richard Leroy Hinds** was born on 23 Aug 1939. He died on 23 Mar 1998.

75. **Roland Leroy Hinds** (Hartley White Hinds, Harvey Wilson Hinds, Alfred White HINDS, John Wellington) was born on 20 Jun 1919 in Toledo, Lucas County, Ohio, USA. He died on 24 Jun 1961 in Grand Canyon, Coconino County, Arizona, USA. He was buried in Sylvania, Lucas County, Ohio, USA.

Roland married **Opal J Whitt** on 2 Aug 1959 in Imperial, California, USA. Opal was born about 1919.

They had the following children:

    161 F   i.   **Judith Ann Hinds** was born on 1 Apr 1942 in Toledo Lucas, Ohio. She died on 23 Jan 2002.

+   162 F   ii.   **Monna Lee Hinds** was born on 24 Mar 1939. She died on 31 Mar 2010.

76. **Elroy Bud Hinds** (Hartley White Hinds, Harvey Wilson Hinds, Alfred White HINDS, John Wellington) was born on 30 Apr 1907 in Toledo, Lucas, Ohio, USA. He died on 3 Nov 1961 in Toledo, Lucas, Ohio.

Elroy married **Luella Bell Woodbury** daughter of John Milton Woodbury and Anna Eliza Cornwill. Luella was born on 18 Jun 1910 in Monroe, Michigan, USA. She died on 5 Oct 1996 in Toledo, Ohio, USA.

They had the following children:

+   163 F   i.   **Charmayne Hinds** .

77. **Bonnie Hinds** (Hartley White Hinds, Harvey Wilson Hinds, Alfred White HINDS, John Wellington)

Bonnie married **Hugo Minor** son of Minor.

They had the following children:

    164 F   i. **Sherry Minor** .

    165 F   ii. **Sally Minor** .

    166 F   iii. **Sandra Minor** .
                    Sandra married **Abromitis** .

    167 F   iv. **Susan Minor** .

79. **Kathryn Augusta Tubbs** (Sarah Elizabeth Sadie Hinds, Lyman Robert Hinds, Alfred White HINDS, John Wellington) was born on 5 Jun 1913 in Riga, Mi. She died on 6 Dec 1977 in Blissfield, Lenawee, Michigan, United States of America.

Kathryn married **Stanley Lawrence ISLEY** on 4 Mar 1934. Stanley was born on 28 Jul 1911 in Blissfield, MI. He died on 10 Aug 1980 in Blissfield, MI.

They had the following children:

    168 M   i. **Private** .

    169 F   ii. **Private** .

+   170 F   iii. **Lou Ann ISLEY** was born on 9 May 1936. She died on 13 Mar 2001.

87. **Lester Earl Hinds** (John White Hinds, Lyman Robert Hinds, Alfred White HINDS, John Wellington) was born about 1901. He died in 1965.

Lester married **Francis Smith** about 1923. Francis was born about 1903.

Lester and Francis had the following children:

    171 F   i. **Martha Ann Hinds**
                    Martha married **Gene Howard Burkalter** about 1946.

    172 F   ii. **Iris Hinds**
                    Iris married **Marshall Deal** about 1944.

104. **Myra Louise Decker** (Vernon Lester Decker, Sarah Louisa Hinds, Alfred White HINDS, John Wellington) was born on 27 Dec 1909 in Toledo, Lucas, Ohio, USA. She died on 2 Aug 1971 in Detroit, Wayne, Michigan, United States.

Myra married **George William Parker** on 27 Jan 1933 in Bowling Green, Licking, Ohio, USA. George was born on 10 Feb 1912 in Toledo, Lucas, Ohio, USA. He died on 5 Feb 2005 in Farmington, Oakland, Michigan. He was buried in Livonia, Wayne County, Michigan, USA.

They had the following children:

173 F   i. **Amy Louise Parker** was born in Indianapolis, Marion, Indiana, USA.

108. **Florence Louisa Sloan** (Florence Ivadell Decker, Sarah Louisa Hinds, Alfred White HINDS, John Wellington) was born on 3 Apr 1920 in Berkey, OH. She died on 7 Nov 1994 in Harrod, Allen, Ohio, USA.

Florence married **Howard Milton Drury** son of Luther Allan Drury and Juliana Priscilla Wingate on 7 Feb 1941 in Lucas, Ohio, USA. Howard was born on 22 Feb 1914 in Allen, Ohio, United States. He died on 20 Jan 1998 in Lima, Allen, Ohio, USA.

They had the following children:

174 M   i. **Timothy Howard Drury** was born on 23 Aug 1943 in Wayne Wayne, Michigan. He died on 19 Jun 2003 in Oceola Twp MI. He was buried in Howell, Livingston County, Michigan, USA. Timothy married **Private** on 27 Mar 1965 in Wayne, Mich.

175 M   ii. **R Drury** .

Sixth Generation

146. **Harry James Rogers** (Hazel May HINDS, Hartley White Hinds, Harvey Wilson Hinds, Alfred White HINDS, John Wellington) was born on 25 May 1928 in Toledo, Lucas County, Ohio. He died on 4 Oct 1977 in Alpena, Alpena, Michigan, USA. He was buried on 6 Oct 1977 in Wilson Twp., Alpena Co., Michigan.

Harry married **Ruth Osenbaugh** daughter of Zenith Sherman Osenbaugh and Iva Irene May Queen Woodbury on 19 Feb 1951 in Monroe, Monroe, Michigan, USA. Ruth was born about 1931 in Toledo, Lucas, Ohio, USA. She died in Toledo, Lucas, Ohio, USA.

They had the following children:

176 F   i. **Donna Rogers** .

177 M   ii. **Michael Rogers** .

178 M   iii. **Gary Rogers** .

179 F   iv. **Vicky Rogers** .

147. **Beverly Jo Hinds** (Warren Edmund Hinds, Hartley White Hinds, Harvey Wilson Hinds, Alfred White HINDS, John Wellington)

Beverly married **Michael Hooks** .

They had the following children:

    180 M   i. **Justin M Hooks**

    181 F   ii. **Jennifer Jo Hooks**

148. **Jeanette Hinds** (Warren Edmund Hinds, Hartley White Hinds, Harvey Wilson Hinds, Alfred White HINDS, John Wellington)

Jeanette married **David Berry**

They had the following children:

    182 M   i. **David Scott Berry** was born on 27 May 1982. He died on 25 May 2008. He was buried in Mena, Polk County, Arkansas, USA.

    183 F   ii. **Stephanie Berry**

    184 F   iii. **Michelle Berry** .

149. **Warren Glenn Hinds** (Warren Edmund Hinds, Hartley White Hinds, Harvey Wilson Hinds, Alfred White HINDS, John Wellington)

Warren married **Barbara**

Warren and Barbara had the following children:

    185 M   i. **Dustin Hinds**

    186 F   ii. **Britany Hinds**

    187 M   iii. **Joshua Hinds**

150. **Jimmy Alan Hinds** (Hartley Wilbur Hinds, Hartley White Hinds, Harvey Wilson Hinds, Alfred White HINDS, John Wellington) was born on 26 Feb 1947 in Toledo, Lucas, Ohio, United States. He died on 27 Jun 2001 in Toledo, Lucas, Ohio, United States of America.

Jimmy married **Patricia Hall** daughter of Melvin Morral Hall and Betty Lorraine Flanders.

They had the following children:

+   188 F   i. **Anna Marie Hinds**

+   189 F   ii. **Evelyn Hinds**

+   190 M   iii. **Jimmy Hinds Jr**

151. **Tommy Gene Hinds** (Hartley Wilbur Hinds, Hartley White Hinds, Harvey Wilson Hinds, Alfred White HINDS, John Wellington) was born on 20 May 1944 in Toledo, Lucas, Ohio, USA. He died on 29 May 2005 in Durant, Hillsborough, Florida.

Tommy married (1) **Grace Beatrice Eckhart** daughter of Ollie Gerald Eckhart and Loretta Mae Nigh in Jan 1962. Grace died in Oct 2005.

They had the following children:

+ 191 F   i. **Debbie Sue Hinds**

    192 M   ii. **Larry Douglass Hinds**

+ 193 F   iii. **Loretta Mae Hinds** was born on 31 Jan 1963. She died on 16 Feb 1985.

Tommy married (2) **Bonnie Lee Reilly** daughter of Robert Elmer Reilly and Mary Yvonne on 7 Jan 1972. Bonnie was born on 6 Jan 1948 in Paterson, Passaic, New Jersey, USA. She died on 18 Mar 2016.

They had the following children:

+ 194 F   iv. **Marjorie Ann Hinds**

+ 195 F   v. **Mary Hinds**

+ 196 M   vi. **Tommy Gene Hinds**

+ 197 F   vii. **Marie Elaine Hinds**

Tommy married (3) **Anna Mae Hardy** daughter of Charles Robert Hardy and Virginia May South.

They had the following children:

+ 198 F   viii. **Diana Hinds**

+ 199 M   ix. **Joe Ray Hinds**

+ 200 F   x. **Terrie L Hinds**

+ 201 M   xi. **Tommy Gene Hinds**

+ 202 F   xii. **Karrie Lynn Hinds**

Tommy married (4) **Donna** . Donna was born in 1962. She died in 2008.

They had the following children:

+ 203 M   xiii. **Richard Mannon**

+ 204 M   xiv. **Donald Mannon**

+ 205 F   xv. **Cynthia Mannon**

152. **Kathleen Ann Hinds** (Hartley Wilbur Hinds, Hartley White Hinds, Harvey Wilson Hinds, Alfred White HINDS, John Wellington) was born in Toledo, Lucas, Ohio, USA.

Kathleen married (1) **James Clark Culbreath 1** son of Julian Pervus Culbreath and Maida Lorel Bickford. James was born on 20 Aug 1940 in Fort Myers, Lee, Florida. He died on 23 Sep 1996 in Bradenton, Manatee, Florida. He was buried in Bradenton, Manatee County, Florida, USA.

They had the following children:

+ 206 M   i. **James Samuel Culbreath**

+ 207 M   ii. **Merton Daniel Culbreath**

+ 208 M   iii. **Timothy Alan Culbreath**

+ 209 F   iv. **Laura Lorel Culbreath**

Kathleen married (2) **Randy Bibbee** .

153. **Hartley William Hinds** (Hartley Wilbur Hinds, Hartley White Hinds, Harvey Wilson Hinds, Alfred White HINDS, John Wellington) was born in Toledo, Lucas, Ohio, USA.

Hartley married **Georgette** .

Hartley and Georgette had the following children:

  210 F   i. **Michelle Danielle Hinds** .

  211 F   ii. **Christine Hinds** .

  212 F   iii. **Hartley William Hinds Jr** .

156. **Nancy Jean Hinds** (Hartley Wilbur Hinds, Hartley White Hinds, Harvey Wilson Hinds, Alfred White HINDS, John Wellington) was born on 8 May 1936 in Toledo, Lucas, Ohio, USA. She died on 28 Mar 1988 in Jefferson, Kentucky.

Nancy married **Freeman Lloyd Coats** son of Dempsey Otho Coats and Easter Aldora on 29 Jan 1953 in Monroe, Michigan, USA. Freeman was born on 9 Mar 1927. He died on 27 Mar 1985 in Louisville, Jefferson, Kentucky, USA.

They had the following children:

+   213 F   i.   **Mary Evelyn Coats**

+   214 M   ii. **Vincent Ray Coats**

+   215 M   iii. **James Eric Coats**

+   216 F   iv. **Karen Fay Coats**

+   217 F   v.   **Donna Jean Coats**

+   218 M   vi. **Freeman Lloyd Coats**

157. **Patsy Louise Hinds** (Hartley Wilbur Hinds, Hartley White Hinds, Harvey Wilson Hinds, Alfred White HINDS, John Wellington) was born on 4 Oct 1934 in Toledo, Lucas, Ohio, USA. She died on 19 Oct 2006 in Frostproof, Polk, Florida, USA.

Patsy married (1) **Paul Morris** . Paul was born on 1 Feb 1932 in Toledo, Lucas, Ohio, USA. He died in 2009.

They had the following children:

+   219 F   i.   **Debra Sue Morris**

+   220 F   ii. **Pamela Louise Morris**

+   221 M   iii. **Paul Sonny Morris**

Patsy married (2) **Robert Lee McKinney** in 1967 in Hendry County, Florida. Robert was born on 4 Jan 1931. He died on 23 Mar 2013.

They had the following children:

    222 M   iv. **Mark McKinney**

+   223 M   v.   **Robert McKinney**

+   224 M   vi. **Ricky Eugene Mckinney**

Patsy married (3) **Carl Lockwood** .

158. **Jerry Eugene Hinds** (Hartley Wilbur Hinds, Hartley White Hinds, Harvey Wilson Hinds, Alfred White HINDS, John Wellington) was born on 24 Mar 1938 in Toledo, Lucas, Ohio, USA. He died on 15 Sep 2005 in Frostproof, Polk, Florida.

Jerry married **Shirley Jean Eckhart** daughter of Ollie Gerald Eckhart and Loretta Mae Nigh about 1960.

They had the following children:

+   225 F   i. **Sherry Hinds**

      226 M   ii. **Jerry Eugene Hinds Jr**
                       Jerry married **Carol Jean Myers** on 15 Sep 1988 in Collier, Florida.

159. **Sandra Sue Hinds** (Hartley Wilbur Hinds, Hartley White Hinds, Harvey Wilson Hinds, Alfred White HINDS, John Wellington) was born in Toledo, Lucas, Ohio, USA.

Sandra married (1) **Dale Earton Lyon** son of Earle Zenas Lyon and Ethel Levina Switser in Jan 1959. Dale was born in St Johnsbury, Caledonia, Vermont, USA.

They had the following children:

+   227 F   i. **Wanda Kay Lyon**

+   228 M   ii. **Randall Kelvin Lyon**

+   229 M   iii. **Donald Ray Lyon**

Sandra married (2) **James Mansel Kurtz** son of Theodore D Kurtz and Shirley Ellen Morris on 15 Apr 1977 in Naples, Collier, Florida

They had the following children:

      230 F   iv. **Jami Sue Kurtz** was born Naples, Collier, Florida, USA.

160. **Richard Leroy Hinds** (Hartley Wilbur Hinds, Hartley White Hinds, Harvey Wilson Hinds, Alfred White HINDS, John Wellington) was born on 23 Aug 1939 in Toledo, Lucas, Ohio, USA. He died on 23 Mar 1998 in Piedmont, Calhoun, Alabama, United States of America,.

Richard married **Shelby Pierce** daughter of Pierce in Jul 1957 in Collier, Florida

Richard and Shelby had the following children:

+   231 M   i. **Richard Hinds Jr**

+   232 F   ii. **Phyllis Hinds** .

162. **Monna Lee Hinds** (Roland Leroy Hinds, Hartley White Hinds, Harvey Wilson Hinds, Alfred White HINDS, John Wellington) was born on 24 Mar 1939. She died on 31 Mar 2010 in Bullhead City, Mohave, Arizona, USA.

Monna married **Richard Barry Licause** on 5 Jul 1958 in Nevada. Richard was born on 21 Sep 1935 in Riverside, California. He died on 9 Aug 2000 in Bentonville, Benton, Arkansas, USA.

They had the following children:

    233 F   i. **Private** .

    234 M   ii. **Roland Leroy Licause** was born in Toledo, Lucas, Ohio, USA.

163. **Charmayne Hinds** (Elroy Bud Hinds, Hartley White Hinds, Harvey Wilson Hinds, Alfred White HINDS, John Wellington).

Charmayne married **Donald Gochenour** .

They had the following children:

    235 M   i. **Jon Donald Gochenour**

    236 M   ii. **Jay Robert Gochenour**

+ 237 F   iii. **Jennifer Ann Gochenour**

    238 M   iv. **Jeffrey Allen Gochenour**

170. **Lou Ann ISLEY** (Kathryn Augusta Tubbs, Sarah Elizabeth Sadie Hinds, Lyman Robert Hinds, Alfred White HINDS, John Wellington) was born on 9 May 1936 in Blissfield, Lenawee, Michigan, USA. She died on 13 Mar 2001 in Hot Springs AK Bur Blissfield, MI. She was buried in Blissfield, Lenawee County, Michigan, USA.

Lou married **Rudolph H. Stahlberg** . Rudolph was born in 1936. He was buried in Blissfield, Lenawee County, Michigan, USA.

They had the following children:

    239 F   i. **LisaRider Stahlberg** .

Seventh Generation

188. **Anna Marie Hinds** (Jimmy Alan Hinds, Hartley Wilbur Hinds, Hartley White Hinds, Harvey Wilson Hinds, Alfred White HINDS, John Wellington

Anna married **Derrick Harris** .

They had the following children:

    240 F   i. **Dakoda Marie Harris**
    241 M   ii. **William Allen Harris**

189. **Evelyn Hinds** (Jimmy Alan Hinds, Hartley Wilbur Hinds, Hartley White Hinds, Harvey Wilson Hinds, Alfred White HINDS, John Wellington)

Evelyn married **Derrick Johnson** .

They had the following children:

    242 F   i. **Erica Johnson** .

    243 F   ii. **Jackie Hinds** .

    244 M   iii. **Devontay Johnson** .

    245 F   iv. **Dedra Johnson** .

    246 M   v. **Derrion Johnson** .

190. **Jimmy Hinds Jr** (Jimmy Alan Hinds, Hartley Wilbur Hinds, Hartley White Hinds, Harvey Wilson Hinds, Alfred White HINDS, John Wellington)

Jimmy married **Wendy** .

They had the following children:

    247 M   i. **Jeremy Hinds** .

    248 M   ii. **Alex Hinds** .

    249 M   iii. **Sam Hinds** .

191. **Debbie Sue Hinds** (Tommy Gene Hinds, Hartley Wilbur Hinds, Hartley White Hinds, Harvey Wilson Hinds, Alfred White HINDS, John Wellington) was born in Los Angeles, California.

Debbie and **Jerry Leroy Cass** had the following child:

+   250 M   i. **Jessie Daniel Cass**

Debbie married (2) **Richard Dane Scott** son of Robert William Scott and Elayne Fae Campbell. Richard was born in Bay Village, Cuyahoga, Ohio, United States.

193. **Loretta Mae Hinds** (Tommy Gene Hinds, Hartley Wilbur Hinds, Hartley White Hinds, Harvey Wilson Hinds, Alfred White HINDS, John Wellington) was born on 31 Jan 1963. She died on 16 Feb 1985.

Loretta married **Dennis James Cass** on 19 Sep 1981 in Clark, Nevada.

They had the following children:

    251 F   i. **Barbara Ann Cass** .

    252 M   ii. **Dennis Cass** .

194. **Marjorie Ann Hinds** (Tommy Gene Hinds, Hartley Wilbur Hinds, Hartley White Hinds, Harvey Wilson Hinds, Alfred White HINDS, John Wellington)

Marjorie married (1) **John Scott.**

She had the following children:

+   253 F   i.   **Brittany Lee Hinds**

195. **Mary Hinds** (Tommy Gene Hinds, Hartley Wilbur Hinds, Hartley White Hinds, Harvey Wilson Hinds, Alfred White HINDS, John Wellington)

She had the following children:

    254 M   i.   **Michael Borowski**

+   255 F   ii.   **Samantha Roberts**

196. **Tommy Gene Hinds** (Tommy Gene Hinds, Hartley Wilbur Hinds, Hartley White Hinds, Harvey Wilson Hinds, Alfred White HINDS, John Wellington)

He had the following children:

    256 F   i.   **Nicole Richmond** .

197. **Marie Elaine Hinds** (Tommy Gene Hinds, Hartley Wilbur Hinds, Hartley White Hinds, Harvey Wilson Hinds, Alfred White HINDS, John Wellington)

Marie had the following children:

    257 F   i.   **Myah Rose Hinds**

    258 M   ii.   **Travis Andrew Priestly**

198. **Diana Hinds** (Tommy Gene Hinds, Hartley Wilbur Hinds, Hartley White Hinds, Harvey Wilson Hinds, Alfred White HINDS, John Wellington)

Diana married **Joseph Norman Vardaman**

They had the following children:

    259 M   i.   **Andrew Joseph Vardaman**

    260 F   ii.   **Roseanna Marlene Vardaman**

+   261 F   iii.   **Shawna Marie Vardaman**

    262 M   iv.   **Garold Joseph Vardaman**

    263 M   v.   **Justin Joe Vardaman**

199. **Joe Ray Hinds** (Tommy Gene Hinds, Hartley Wilbur Hinds, Hartley White Hinds, Harvey Wilson Hinds, Alfred White HINDS, John Wellington)

He had the following children:

   264 F   i. **Cheyenne Hinds** .

   265 F   ii. **Belladonna Hinds** .

200. **Terrie L Hinds** (Tommy Gene Hinds, Hartley Wilbur Hinds, Hartley White Hinds, Harvey Wilson Hinds, Alfred White HINDS, John Wellington)

Terrie married **Brad J Perry** on 28 Feb 1994.

They had the following children:

   266 M   i. **Jacob Perry**

   267 M   ii. **Bradley Perry**

   268 F   iii. **Elizabeth Perry**

   269 F   iv. **Liza Perry**

201. **Tommy Gene Hinds** (Tommy Gene Hinds, Hartley Wilbur Hinds, Hartley White Hinds, Harvey Wilson Hinds, Alfred White HINDS, John Wellington)

Tommy married (1) **Angela Christine Rink** daughter of Samuel Rink and Patricia K. Rink on 21 May 2002 in Bunker Hill, Miami, Indiana, USA.

Tommy married (2) **Misty** .

They had the following children:

   270 F   i. **Diana Rae Hinds** .

202. **Karrie Lynn Hinds** (Tommy Gene Hinds, Hartley Wilbur Hinds, Hartley White Hinds, Harvey Wilson Hinds, Alfred White HINDS, John Wellington)

She had the following children:

   271 M   i. **Waylon Hunter Clary**

   272 F   ii. **Amber Jean Cross**

   273 F   iii. **Anastasia Chevelle Cross**

203. **Richard Mannon** (Tommy Gene Hinds, Hartley Wilbur Hinds, Hartley White Hinds, Harvey Wilson Hinds, Alfred White HINDS, John Wellington)

He had the following children:

    274 F   i. **Emily Kay Mannon** .

204. **Donald Mannon** (Tommy Gene Hinds, Hartley Wilbur Hinds, Hartley White Hinds, Harvey Wilson Hinds, Alfred White HINDS, John Wellington)

Donald married **Amanda Paupard.**

They had the following children:

    275 F   i. **Kaylee Paupard**

    276 F   ii. **Alexa Paupard**

    277 F   iii. **Alyssa Paupard**

205. **Cynthia Mannon** (Tommy Gene Hinds, Hartley Wilbur Hinds, Hartley White Hinds, Harvey Wilson Hinds, Alfred White HINDS, John Wellington)

She had the following children:

    278 M   i. **Joshawa Friesel**

    279 F   ii. **Julie Friesel**

    280 M   iii. **James Mannon**

206. **James Samuel Culbreath** (Kathleen Ann Hinds, Hartley Wilbur Hinds, Hartley White Hinds, Harvey Wilson Hinds, Alfred White HINDS, John Wellington)

James married **Glenda K Fuller** on 26 Nov 1994 in Stearns, Minnesota, USA

They had the following children:

+   281 F   i. **Jami Culbreath**

    282 F   ii. **Kathleen Culbreath**

207. **Merton Daniel Culbreath** (Kathleen Ann Hinds, Hartley Wilbur Hinds, Hartley White Hinds, Harvey Wilson Hinds, Alfred White HINDS, John Wellington) was born in Naples, Collier, Florida, USA.

Merton married (1) **Monich** .

They had the following children:

    283 M   i. **Jonathan Culbreath**.

Merton married (2) **Danielle Lori Davies** . Danielle was born in Boynton Beach,

FL.

They had the following children:

284 M   ii. **James Clark Culbreath II** was born in West Palm Beach, Palm Beach, Florida, USA.

208. **Timothy Alan Culbreath** (Kathleen Ann Hinds, Hartley Wilbur Hinds, Hartley White Hinds, Harvey Wilson Hinds, Alfred White HINDS, John Wellington) was born in Naples, Collier, Florida, USA.

Timothy married **Joyce Renea King** on 5 Mar 1988 in Wellburn, FL. Joyce was born in Russelville, AL.

They had the following children:

285 M   i. **Christopher Lee Culbreath** was born in Naples, Collier, Florida, USA.

+ 286 M   ii. **Justin Scott Culbreath**

287 M   iii. **Mark Alan Culbreath** was born in Toledo, Lucas, Ohio, USA.

209. **Laura Lorel Culbreath** (Kathleen Ann Hinds, Hartley Wilbur Hinds, Hartley White Hinds, Harvey Wilson Hinds, Alfred White HINDS, John Wellington) was born in Naples, Collier, Florida, USA.

Laura married **Harry Walter Alderman II** son of Harry Alderman on 18 Nov 1985 in Naples, Collier, Florida, USA. Harry was born in Fort Myers, Lee, FL.

They had the following children:

288 M   i. **Randall Walter Alderman** was born in Gainesville, Alachua, FL.

289 M   ii. **Scott Neil Alderman** was born in Jacksonville, Duval, Florida, USA.
Scott married **Bridgette Chittenden**

290 M   iii. **David Allen Alderman** was born in Naples, Collier, Florida, USA.

213. **Mary Evelyn Coats** (Nancy Jean Hinds, Hartley Wilbur Hinds, Hartley White Hinds, Harvey Wilson Hinds, Alfred White HINDS, John Wellington) was born in Tampa, Hillsborough, Florida, USA.

Mary married (1) **Roy E Casey** .

They had the following children:

+ 291 M   i. **Gregory Allan Coats**

+ 292 F   ii. **Misty Dawn Coats**

Mary married (2) **Jose Carmen Melendez** in Palmyra, Harrison, Indiana, USA.

Mary married (3) **Fulgencio Perez** . Fulgencio was born in Puerto Rico.

They had the following children:

+   293 M   iii. **Billy Joe Perez**

+   294 F   iv. **Maryanne Perez**

214. **Vincent Ray Coats** (Nancy Jean Hinds, Hartley Wilbur Hinds, Hartley White Hinds, Harvey Wilson Hinds, Alfred White HINDS, John Wellington) was born in Salem, Delaware, Indiana, USA.

     He had the following children:

     295 M   i. **Travis Coats**

215. **James Eric Coats** (Nancy Jean Hinds, Hartley Wilbur Hinds, Hartley White Hinds, Harvey Wilson Hinds, Alfred White HINDS, John Wellington) was born in Salem, Delaware, Indiana, USA.
James married (1) **Ann Louise Boyce** on 16 Dec 1989 in Beaufort, SC. Ann was born in Charleston, SC.

     He had the following children:

     296 M   i. **James Eric Coats Jr** was born in Orlando, Brevard, Florida, USA.

216. **Karen Fay Coats** (Nancy Jean Hinds, Hartley Wilbur Hinds, Hartley White Hinds, Harvey Wilson Hinds, Alfred White HINDS, John Wellington) was born in Tampa, Hillsborough, Florida, USA.

     Karen married (1) **Allan Casey** .

     They had the following children:

     297 M   i. **Michael Lynn Coats** was born in Salem, Delaware, Indiana, USA.

     Karen married (2) **Thomas Edward Dudley** . Thomas was born in Indiana, USA.

     They had the following children:

     298 M   ii. **Bradley Edward Dudley** was born in Salem, Delaware, Indiana, USA.

     299 F   iii. **Alisa Elaine Dudley** was born in Clewiston, FL.

Karen married (3) **Jeffery Harrell** .

They had the following children:

   300 M   iv. **Jeremy Harrell**

217. **Donna Jean Coats** (Nancy Jean Hinds, Hartley Wilbur Hinds, Hartley White Hinds, Harvey Wilson Hinds, Alfred White HINDS, John Wellington) was born in Salem, Delaware, Indiana, USA.

Donna married (1) **Douglas Blaine Lee** on 21 Aug 1972 in Borden, IN.

They had the following children:

   301 F   i. **Bonnie Sue Lee** was born in Clewiston, FL.

   302 F   ii. **Michelle Kaye Lee** was born in Salem, Delaware, Indiana, USA.

   303 F   iii. **Karen Ann Lee** was born in Borden, IN.

Donna married (2) **Michael Etheridge Day** on 10 Oct 1984 in Albany, GA.

218. **Freeman Lloyd Coats** (Nancy Jean Hinds, Hartley Wilbur Hinds, Hartley White Hinds, Harvey Wilson Hinds, Alfred White HINDS, John Wellington) was born in Tampa, Hillsborough, Florida, USA.

Freeman married **Shirley Washam** on 1 Sep 1990 in Pekin, Washington, Indiana, USA. Shirley was born in Ohio.

They had the following children:

+   304 F   i. **Jennifer Coats** .

+   305 M   ii. **Steven Coats**

219. **Debra Sue Morris** (Patsy Louise Hinds, Hartley Wilbur Hinds, Hartley White Hinds, Harvey Wilson Hinds, Alfred White HINDS, John Wellington) was born in Fort Benning, GA.

Debra married (1) **Larry L. Sims** in 1969. Larry was born in Hogansville, Troup, Georgia, USA.

They had the following children:

   306 M   i. **Jerry L. Sims** was born in Fort Myers, Lee, FL.

   307 F   ii. **Tammy L. Sims** was born in Punta Gorda, Charlotte, Florida, USA.

+   308 M   iii. **Larry L. Sims**.

+ 309 M iv. **Barry L. Sims**

Debra married (2) **Roy F. Curry** on 6 Dec 1982.

220. **Pamela Louise Morris** (Patsy Louise Hinds, Hartley Wilbur Hinds, Hartley White Hinds, Harvey Wilson Hinds, Alfred White HINDS, John Wellington).

Pamela married **James Eugene Lavelle** on 11 Aug 1971 in Lee, Florida.

They had the following children:

310 F i. **Sherry Lavelle** .

221. **Paul Sonny Morris** (Patsy Louise Hinds, Hartley Wilbur Hinds, Hartley White Hinds, Harvey Wilson Hinds, Alfred White HINDS, John Wellington)

Paul married **Denise Miller** in 1970.

They had the following children:

311 F i. **Mariah G Morris** .

312 M ii. **Paul F Morris**

313 F iii. **Valerie Morris** .

223. **Robert McKinney** (Patsy Louise Hinds, Hartley Wilbur Hinds, Hartley White Hinds, Harvey Wilson Hinds, Alfred White HINDS, John Wellington)
He had the following children:

314 M i. **Michael McKinney** .

315 M ii. **Bobby Lee McKinney** .

316 M iii. **Robbie McKinney** .

317 M iv. **Danial McKinney** .

224. **Ricky Eugene Mckinney** (Patsy Louise Hinds, Hartley Wilbur Hinds, Hartley White Hinds, Harvey Wilson Hinds, Alfred White HINDS, John Wellington)

Ricky married **Kathy Ileen Dinehart** daughter of Leslie L. Dinehart and Margaret Bergman on 19 Aug 1977 in Lee, Florida. Kathy was born on 3 Sep 1958. She died on 14 Sep 2000 in S&S Memorial Hospital,Penn Yan,NY.

They had the following children:

318 M i. **Ricky Alan McKinney Jr.** .

319 F   ii. **Misty Dawn McKinney** .

225. **Sherry Hinds** (Jerry Eugene Hinds, Hartley Wilbur Hinds, Hartley White Hinds, Harvey Wilson Hinds, Alfred White HINDS, John Wellington)

Sherry had the following children:

320 F   i. **Bobby Hinds**

\+   321 F   ii. **Darlene Hinds**

\+   322 F   iii. **Charlene Lynn Hinds**

227. **Wanda Kay Lyon** (Sandra Sue Hinds, Hartley Wilbur Hinds, Hartley White Hinds, Harvey Wilson Hinds, Alfred White HINDS, John Wellington) was born in Naples, Collier, Florida, USA.

Wanda married (1) **Kim Allen** son of William Benjamin Allen on 19 Aug 1983 in Naples, Collier, Florida, USA. Kim was born in Bath, Steuben, NY.

Wanda married (2) **Jackie Lee Loving** .

They had the following children:

\+   323 M   i. **Daniel Lee Allen**

\+   324 M   ii. **Jennifer Lynn Allen**

228.   **Randall Kelvin Lyon** (Sandra Sue Hinds, Hartley Wilbur Hinds, Hartley White Hinds, Harvey Wilson Hinds, Alfred White HINDS, John Wellington) in Naples, Collier, Florida, USA.

Randall married (1) **Alene Wilhelmina Lynk** daughter of Lynk on 23 Apr 1980 in Naples, Collier, Florida, United States of America.

Randall married (2) **Lisa Lynn Epperson** daughter of James O Epperson and Jane Estes on 20 Jun 1997 in Naples, Collier, Florida, USA. Lisa was born in Winchester, Clark, Kentucky, USA.

Randall adopted Jacqulyn

\+   325 F   i. **Jacqulyn Renae Cheri Lyon**

Randall married (3) **Rhonda Lynn Crouch** daughter of James Rudolph Crouch and Margaret Evans on 10 Aug 2001 in Collier, Florida. Rhonda was born in East St. Louis, St. Clair, IL.

229. **Donald Ray Lyon** (Sandra Sue Hinds, Hartley Wilbur Hinds, Hartley White Hinds, Harvey Wilson Hinds, Alfred White HINDS, John Wellington) was born in Bowling Green, OH.

Donald married **Dawn Annette Scott** daughter of Andrew Mclachlan Scott and Reva Van Hoose on 15 Nov 1976 in Naples, Collier, Florida, USA. Dawn was born in Los Angeles, California, USA.

They had the following children:

    326 M   i. **Donald Ray Lyon** was born in Naples, Collier, Florida, USA.

    327 F   ii. **Amy Sue Lyon** was born in Naples, Collier, Florida, USA.

    231.   **Richard Hinds Jr** (Richard Leroy Hinds, Hartley Wilbur Hinds, Hartley White Hinds, Harvey Wilson Hinds, Alfred White HINDS, John Wellington)

Richard married (1) **Lisa Bramlett** .

They had the following children:

    328 M   i. **Kyle Richard Hinds**

    329 F   ii. **Mandi Megan Hinds**

    330 F   iii. **Leila Hinds**
              Leila married **Jeff Reaves** on 5 Jul 2016.

Richard married (2) **Sheila Baker**

232. **Phyllis Hinds** (Richard Leroy Hinds, Hartley Wilbur Hinds, Hartley White Hinds, Harvey Wilson Hinds, Alfred White HINDS, John Wellington).

Phyllis married **Jim Wenrich** .

They had the following children:

    331 M   i. **Tyler Wenrich** .

    332 M   ii. **Travis Wenrich** .

237. **Jennifer Ann Gochenour** (Charmayne Hinds, Elroy Bud Hinds, Hartley White Hinds, Harvey Wilson Hinds, Alfred White HINDS, John Wellington).

Jennifer married **Douglas Finch** .

They had the following children:

    333 F   i. **Kaleigh Ashton Finch** .

Eighth Generation

250. **Jessie Daniel Cass** (Debbie Sue Hinds, Tommy Gene Hinds, Hartley Wilbur Hinds, Hartley White Hinds, Harvey Wilson Hinds, Alfred White HINDS, John Wellington)

Jessie married (1) **Karen Cooper** .

They had the following children:

334 M   i.   **Aiden James Cass** was born in Riverside, California.

Jessie married (2) **Megan Renee Cullars** .

They had the following children:

335 F   ii.   **Karlee Dee Cass** was born on 10 Apr 2014. She died on 23 Jul 2015.

336 F   iii.   **Heidi Iris Cass**

337 F   iv.   **Isabella ReLyn Cass**

338 F   v.   **Emma Loretta Cass**

253. **Brittany Lee Hinds** (Marjorie Ann Hinds, Tommy Gene Hinds, Hartley Wilbur Hinds, Hartley White Hinds, Harvey Wilson Hinds, Alfred White HINDS, John Wellington)

She had the following children:

339 M   i.   **Dylan Jeffery Hinds**

255. **Samantha Roberts** (Mary Hinds, Tommy Gene Hinds, Hartley Wilbur Hinds, Hartley White Hinds, Harvey Wilson Hinds, Alfred White HINDS, John Wellington)

She had the following children:

340 F   i.   **Gia Roberts** .

261. **Shawna Marie Vardaman** (Diana Hinds, Tommy Gene Hinds, Hartley Wilbur Hinds, Hartley White Hinds, Harvey Wilson Hinds, Alfred White HINDS, John Wellington).

Shawna married **Tommy Lee Falkenburg** .

They had the following children:

341 F   i.   **MaKenna Mai Falkenburg**

281. **Jami Culbreath** (James Samuel Culbreath, Kathleen Ann Hinds, Hartley Wilbur Hinds, Hartley White Hinds, Harvey Wilson Hinds, Alfred White HINDS, John Wellington)

Jami married **Anthony Frost** .

They had the following children:

    342 F   i. **Alayna Frost** .

    343 M   ii. **David Frost** .

    344 F   iii. **Chasity Frost** .

286. **Justin Scott Culbreath** (Timothy Alan Culbreath, Kathleen Ann Hinds, Hartley Wilbur Hinds, Hartley White Hinds, Harvey Wilson Hinds, Alfred White HINDS, John Wellington) was born in Toledo, Lucas, Ohio, USA.

Justin married **Sarah** .

They had the following children:

    345 M   i. **Ian Scott Culbreath**

291. **Gregory Allan Coats** (Mary Evelyn Coats, Nancy Jean Hinds, Hartley Wilbur Hinds, Hartley White Hinds, Harvey Wilson Hinds, Alfred White HINDS, John Wellington) was born in Clewiston, FL.

Gregory married (1) **Kelly Bolen** .

They had the following children:

    346 F   i. **Taylor Bolen** .

Gregory married (2) **Angela Caudill** .

They had the following children:

    347 F   ii. **Nancy Coats** .

    348 F   iii. **Jorydon Coats** .

    349 F   iv. **Autumn Coats** .

    350 M   v. **Brandon Coats** .

Gregory married (3) **Danielle Keen** .

They had the following children:

    351 F   vi. **Sofia Coats** .

292. **Misty Dawn Coats** (Mary Evelyn Coats, Nancy Jean Hinds, Hartley Wilbur Hinds, Hartley White Hinds, Harvey Wilson Hinds, Alfred White HINDS, John Wellington) was born in Salem, Delaware, Indiana, USA.

Misty married (1) **Keith D. Payne** son of Robert and Michelle on 30 Apr 1994 in Depauw, Harrison, Indiana, USA. Keith was born in KENTUCKY.

They had the following children:

    352 F   i. **Courtney Payne** .

+   353 M   ii. **Justin Payne** .

    354 M   iii. **Nicholas Payne** .
                 Nicholas married **Kayla Guinn** .

Misty married (2) **Michael Long** .

They had the following children:

+   355 M   iv. **Michael Long** .

293. **Billy Joe Perez** (Mary Evelyn Coats, Nancy Jean Hinds, Hartley Wilbur Hinds, Hartley White Hinds, Harvey Wilson Hinds, Alfred White HINDS, John Wellington) was born in Clewiston, FL.

Billy married (1) **Melissa DeHoney** .

They had the following children:

    356 M   i. **Joseph Dehoney** .

Billy married (2) **Dana W** .

They had the following children:

    357 M   ii. **Waylon Perez** .

    358 M   iii. **Wyatt Perez** .

294. **Maryanne Perez** (Mary Evelyn Coats, Nancy Jean Hinds, Hartley Wilbur Hinds, Hartley White Hinds, Harvey Wilson Hinds, Alfred White HINDS, John Wellington) was born in Clewiston, FL.

Maryanne married (1) **Luis A. Granados** on 1 Jul 1998 in Corydon, Harrison,

Indiana, USA. Luis was born in El Savador.

They had the following children:

359 F   i. **Mikayla Granados** .

Maryanne married (2) **Markeith Pope** .

They had the following children:

360 F   ii. **Mary Bethe Granados** .

Maryanne married (3) **Juan Lopez** .

They had the following children:

361 F   iii. **Katherin Cernia Perez** .

Maryanne married (4) **Jose Banilla** .

They had the following children:

362 M   iv. **Jonathan Perez** .

Maryanne married (5) **Miguel Chavez** on 14 Jun 2010 in Dubois, Indiana, USA.

They had the following children:

363 M   v. **Edward Chavez** .

364 F   vi. **Elizabeth Chavez** .

365 M   vii. **Miguel Chavez** .

304. **Jennifer Coats** (Freeman Lloyd Coats, Nancy Jean Hinds, Hartley Wilbur Hinds, Hartley White Hinds, Harvey Wilson Hinds, Alfred White HINDS, John Wellington).

Jennifer married **Mark Winn** .

They had the following children:

366 M   i. **Eli Winn**

305. **Steven Coats** (Freeman Lloyd Coats, Nancy Jean Hinds, Hartley Wilbur Hinds, Hartley White Hinds, Harvey Wilson Hinds, Alfred White HINDS, John Wellington)

Steven married **Jayme** .

They had the following children:

    367 F   i. **Emily Coats** .

    368 M   ii. **Blake Coats** .

    369 F   iii. **Mackinze Coats** .

308. **Larry L. Sims** (Debra Sue Morris, Patsy Louise Hinds, Hartley Wilbur Hinds, Hartley White Hinds, Harvey Wilson Hinds, Alfred White HINDS, John Wellington) was born in Fort Myers, Lee, FL.

Larry married **Renee Rich** .

They had the following children:

    370 F   i. **Samantha Blair Sims**

    371 M   ii. **Larry L. Sims**

309. **Barry L. Sims** (Debra Sue Morris, Patsy Louise Hinds, Hartley Wilbur Hinds, Hartley White Hinds, Harvey Wilson Hinds, Alfred White HINDS, John Wellington) was born in Fort Myers, Lee, FL.

Barry married **Lisa Padrone** .

They had the following children:

    372 F   i. **Brittney L. Sims**

321. **Darlene Hinds** (Sherry Hinds, Jerry Eugene Hinds, Hartley Wilbur Hinds, Hartley White Hinds, Harvey Wilson Hinds, Alfred White HINDS, John Wellington)

She had the following children:

    373 F   i. **Gracie Lynn Hinds** .

322. **Charlene Lynn Hinds** (Sherry Hinds, Jerry Eugene Hinds, Hartley Wilbur Hinds, Hartley White Hinds, Harvey Wilson Hinds, Alfred White HINDS, John Wellington)

Charlene married **Joseph Wayne Williams** .

They had the following children:

    374 M   i. **Brandon Lee Eugene Williams**

    375 F   ii. **Kara Ann Williams**

323. **Daniel Lee Allen** (Wanda Kay Lyon, Sandra Sue Hinds, Hartley Wilbur Hinds, Hartley White Hinds, Harvey Wilson Hinds, Alfred White HINDS, John Wellington)

was born in Naples, Collier, Florida, USA.

He had the following children:

376 M	i.	**Alex Colton Allen** was born in Greenville, SC.
377 M	ii.	**Aiden Wyatt Allen** was born in Greenville, SC.
378 F	iii.	**Riley Jo Allen** was born in Easley, SC.

324. **Jennifer Lynn Allen** (Wanda Kay Lyon, Sandra Sue Hinds, Hartley Wilbur Hinds, Hartley White Hinds, Harvey Wilson Hinds, Alfred White HINDS, John Wellington) was born on 4 Feb 1981 in Naples, Collier, Florida, USA.

He had the following children:

379 F	i.	**Adalyn Kae Allen** was born in Greenville, SC.
380 M	ii.	**Robert Landyn Gonzalez** was born in Greenville, SC.
381 M	iii.	**Andrew Shane Allen** was born in Greenville, SC.

325. **Jacqulyn Renae Cheri Lyon** (Randall Kelvin Lyon, Sandra Sue Hinds, Hartley Wilbur Hinds, Hartley White Hinds, Harvey Wilson Hinds, Alfred White HINDS, John Wellington) was born in Lexington, Fayette County, KY.

Jacqulyn married **Kelan R Thompson** son of Neal Thompson and Antonine on 30 Nov 2013.

They had the following children:

| 382 F | i. | **Mira Eden Thompson** was born in Oshkosh, Winnebago, Wisconsin, USA. |

Ninth Generation

353. **Justin Payne** (Misty Dawn Coats, Mary Evelyn Coats, Nancy Jean Hinds, Hartley Wilbur Hinds, Hartley White Hinds, Harvey Wilson Hinds, Alfred White HINDS, John Wellington).

Justin married **Allie Taylor** .

They had the following children:

| 383 F | i. | **Carmen Payne** . |
| 384 F | ii. | **Claire Payne** . |

355. **Michael Long** (Misty Dawn Coats, Mary Evelyn Coats, Nancy Jean Hinds, Hartley

Wilbur Hinds, Hartley White Hinds, Harvey Wilson Hinds, Alfred White HINDS, John Wellington).

Michael married **Samantha Fox** .

They had the following children:

385 F   i. **Mia Long** .

386 M   ii. **Mason Bowen** .

Descendants of Daniel Woodbury

First Generation

1. **Daniel Woodbury** was born on 30 May 1791 in Bridport, Addison, Vermont, United States. He died on 8 Aug 1878 in Whiteford, Monroe, Michigan, USA.

Daniel married **Experience Sarah Durkee** daughter of Phineas Durkee and Phebe Pearl on 10 Jan 1810 in Orwell, Addison, Vermont, USA. Experience was born in 1796 in , , New York, USA. She died on 14 May 1872 in Whiteford, Monroe, Michigan, USA.

They had the following children:

	2 M	i.	**Harvey Woodbury** was born about 1838 in Ohio.
+	3 M	ii.	**Joseph Woodbury** was born on 15 Mar 1835. He died on 1 Nov 1908.
+	4 M	iii.	**Lyman Woodbury** was born on 1 Jul 1832. He died on 14 Jan 1903.
	5 F	iv.	**Rosa Woodbury** was born about 1849 in Michigan.
	6 F	v.	**Sarah Woodbury** was born in 1846 in Whiteford, Monroe, Michigan, USA. She died in 1916.
	7 M	vi.	**Eli Woodbury** was born on 13 Mar 1839 in , Portage, Ohio, USA. He died on 4 Sep 1915 in Lennawee, , Michigan, USA. He was buried in Blissfield Cem, Blissfield, Mi. Eli married **Rosaltha Black** daughter of Isaac Black and Electra on 16 Oct 1866 in Lambertville, Monroe, Michigan, USA. Rosaltha was born in May 1850 in Michigan. She died on 2 Dec 1932 in Blissfield, MI.
+	8 M	vii.	**Albert Joseph Woodbury** was born on 24 Sep 1827. He died on 1 Jul 1901.
+	9 F	viii.	**Anna Woodbury** was born on 16 Jan 1815. She died on 7 Oct 1895.
	10 F	ix.	**Lucy Woodbury** was born in 1813.
	11 M	x.	**Daniel Woodbury** was born in 1810 in , , Vermont, USA. He died on 27 Oct 1879 in Whiteford, Monroe, Michigan, USA.
+	12 M	xi.	**David Woodbury** was born on 4 Oct 1820. He died on 9 Apr 1894.
	13 F	xii.	**Eliza Amanda Woodbury** was born on 16 Nov 1819 in Vermont, USA. She died on 7 Oct 1895 in Whiteford, Monroe, Michigan,

USA. She was buried in Union Cem Whiteford, MI.
Eliza married **William Henry Givens** on 19 Aug 1837. William was born on 19 Mar 1809 in Ireland. He died on 4 Mar 1892 in Whiteford, Monroe, Michigan, USA. He was buried in union Cem. Whiteford, Mi.

+   14 F   xiii.   **Polly S Woodbury** was born in 1817. She died about 1880.

Second Generation

3. **Joseph Woodbury** (Daniel) was born on 15 Mar 1835 in , Portage, Ohio, USA. He died on 1 Nov 1908 in Whiteford, Monroe, Michigan, USA. He was buried in union Cem. Whiteford, Mi.

Joseph married **Rosina Burnham** daughter of François Bonhomme and Marguerite Gee in 1862. Rosina was born on 16 Jun 1842 in Michigan. She died after 1930. She was buried in Lambertville, Monroe County, Michigan, USA.

They had the following children:

   15 F   i.   **Mary Woodbury** was born in Apr 1882 in Michigan.

+   16 F   ii.   **Hannah Woodbury** was born on 21 Jan 1876. She died on 17 Apr 1946.

   17 M   iii.   **John Woodbury** was born in May 1885 in Michigan.

   18 M   iv.   **Henry Woodbury** was born in Dec 1890 in Michigan.

   19 F   v.   **Ora Woodbury** was born in Nov 1888 in Ohio.

+   20 F   vi.   **Mary Jane Woodbury** was born on 10 Feb 1863. She died on 6 Jan 1888.

+   21 M   vii.   **Henry Harrison Woodbury** was born in May 1861. He died on 1 Nov 1935.

   22 M   viii.   **Alexander Woodbury** was born in Jun 1865 in Whiteford twp., Monroe Co., Michigan. He died on 4 Apr 1951 in Ann Arbor, Michigan.

+   23 F   ix.   **Lucille (Madeline) Woodbury** was born on 21 Feb 1869. She died on 17 Dec 1948.

+   24 M   x.   **Julius Woodbury** was born in Sep 1868. He died on 24 Jan 1956.

4. **Lyman Woodbury** (Daniel) was born on 1 Jul 1832 in Portage, Ohio, USA. He died on 14 Jan 1903 in Blissfield, Coshocton, Ohio, USA. He was buried in Blissfield, Lenawee County, Michigan, USA.

Lyman married **Margaret Halimony** daughter of Joseph Halimony and Dora Sahl on 11 Nov 1853 in Lucas County, Ohio. Margaret was born on 1 Apr 1836 in Germany. She died on 21 Oct 1920 in Blissfield, Lenawee Cnty, MI.

They had the following children:

       25 F   i. **Mary Woodbury** was born in 1868.

+   26 M   ii. **George Elmer Woodbury** was born on 17 Sep 1871. He died on 7 Apr 1946.

+   27 F   iii. **Maggie A Woodbury** was born about 1874.

       28 F   iv. **Emma Woodbury** was born in 1857 in Michigan, USA.

+   29 F   v. **Ella M. Woodbury** was born in Dec 1864. She died on 3 May 1902.

+   30 F   vi. **Addie Cordelia Woodbury** was born about 1866.

8. **Albert Joseph Woodbury** (Daniel) was born on 24 Sep 1827 in Portage, Ohio, USA. He died on 1 Jul 1901 in Toledo, Lucas, Ohio, USA. He was buried in Whiteford Union Cemetery, Lambertville, Michigan.

Albert married **Eliza Reed** daughter of John Reed and Mary S. Roby in 1847. Eliza was born about 1830 in Ohio. She died on 18 Mar 1891 in Whiteford, Monroe Michigan. She was buried in Lambertville, Monroe County, Michigan, USA.

They had the following children:

+   31 M   i. **Harvey Woodbury** was born on 12 Apr 1859. He died on 27 Dec 1943.

       32 M   ii. **Albert Woodbury Jr.** was born on 20 Oct 1861 in OH. He died on 26 Jan 1907 in Toledo, Lucas, Ohio, USA.
Albert married (1) **Emma Orner** on 11 Oct 1901 in Monroe, Monroe, Michigan, USA. Emma was born in Indiana, USA.
Albert married (2) **Sarah Roberts** on 12 Jan 1893.

       33 M   iii. **Henry Woodbury** was born about 1858 in Ohio.

+   34 F   iv. **Sarah Ann Woodbury** was born on 15 Nov 1857. She died on 10 Oct 1916.

       35 M   v. **John H. Woodbury** was born in 1846 in OH.

+   36 F   vi. **Martha Jane WOODBURY** was born on 18 Jun 1847. She died on 20 Apr 1932.

37 M   vii. **William Woodbury** was born in 1852 in OH.

9. **Anna Woodbury** (Daniel) was born on 16 Jan 1815 in Orwell, Addison, Vermont, United States. She died on 7 Oct 1895 in Whiteford, Michigan, USA. She was buried in Union Cem Whiteford, MI.

Anna married **Avery Otis Noble** son of Solomon Noble and Lois Thomas on 19 Oct 1834 in Ravenna, Portage, Ohio, USA. Avery was born on 3 Nov 1803 in Blandford, Mass. He died on 10 Jul 1884 in Whiteford, Michigan, USA.

They had the following children:

    38 F   i. **Ann Angenette Noble** was born on 4 Feb 1850 in Ravenna.

    39 F   ii. **Laura Elizabeth Noble** was born on 24 Jun 1848 in Ravenna, Portage, Ohio.

    40 F   iii. **Lois Eliza Noble** was born on 28 Apr 1838 in Ravenna, Portage, Ohio. She died on 15 Oct 1838 in Ravenna, Portage, Ohio.

    41 F   iv. **Maria Eliza Noble** was born on 3 Oct 1845 in Ravenna, Portage, Ohio.

    42 F   v. **Sarah Adeline Noble** was born on 14 Jun 1841 in Ravenna.

+   43 M   vi. **Benjamin Franklin Noble** was born on 4 Sep 1839. He died about 1915.

    44 F   vii. **Chloe Julia Noble** was born on 4 Jul 1843 in Ravenna.

    45 F   viii. **Mannie Noble** was born in 1844 in Portage, Ohio, USA.

12. **David Woodbury** (Daniel) was born on 4 Oct 1820 in , Portage, Ohio, USA. He died on 9 Apr 1894 in Lennawee, , Michigan, USA. He was buried in Oakwood Cem, Adrian, MI.

David married (1) **Louisa Amelia Monroe** daughter of Merrick Alexander Monroe and Catherine A. Miles in Jan 1871. Louisa was born on 11 Jan 1837 in Farrington, Berkshire, England. She died on 18 Mar 1909 in Jasper, Lenawee, Michigan, USA. She was buried in Ridgeville Cemetery, Jasper, Lenawee Co., Michigan.

They had the following children:

    46 M   i. **George Woodbury Hathaway** was born on 7 Sep 1874 in Monroe, Michigan, USA. He died on 12 Jun 1956 in Ypsilanti, Washtenaw, Michigan, USA.
       George married in 1918 in Twin Falls, Idaho.

David married (2) **Sarah Scott** in 1871 in Deerfield, Isabella, Michigan, USA. Sarah was born in 1853 in Michigan, USA.

They had the following children:

> 47 M   ii.   **Jessie Woodbury** was born in 1881 in Deerfield, MI. He died on 15 Jul 1901 in Adrian, Michigan, USA.
>
> 48 M   iii.   **Ora Woodbury** was born in 1880.
>
> 49 M   iv.   **David Woodbury** was born about 1879 in Michigan.

David married (3) **Rachel M. Witzel** on 13 Apr 1844 in Trumbull, Ashtabula, Ohio, USA. Rachel was born before 1824.

They had the following children:

> +   50 F   v.   **Matilda Woodbury** was born in 1848. She died on 1 Jan 1908.
>
> +   51 F   vi.   **Martha Woodbury** was born on 4 Nov 1846. She died on 23 Sep 1906.

David married (4) **Julianna Bodett** daughter of J Eli Bodett and Josette Proux on 18 Aug 1856 in Wellsville, MI. Julianna was born in 1818 in St Hyacinthe, , Quebec, Canada. She died in 1870 in Wellsville, Michigan, United States.

They had the following children:

> +   52 M   vii.   **John Milton Woodbury** was born on 27 Sep 1870. He died on 11 Feb 1943.

David married (5) **Susan M Weatherby** on 5 Jul 1887 in Palmyra, Lenawee, Michigan, USA. Susan was born about 1833 in New York.

14. **Polly S Woodbury** (Daniel) was born in 1817 in Orwell, Addison, Vermont, USA. She died about 1880 in Whiteford, Monroe, Michigan, USA. She was buried in Union Cem Whiteford, MI.

Polly married **Eleazer Bowers** on 29 Mar 1832 in Portage County Oh. Eleazer was born about 1809 in New York, USA. He died before 1870 in Whiteford, Monroe, Michigan, USA. He was buried in Union Cemetery, Whiteford, MI.

They had the following children:

> +   53 M   i.   **Edwin Bowers** was born in Jun 1842. He died on 12 Dec 1922.
>
> 54 F   ii.   **Amanda Bowers** was born in 1847 in Whiteford, Monroe, Michigan, USA.
>
> 55 M   iii.   **Louis Samuel Bowers** was born in 1835 in Portage, Ohio, USA.
>
> 56 M   iv.   **Frederick Bowers** was born about 1837 in Ohio. He died on 1 Jun 1862 in Pittsburg Landing, Tennessee, USA.

Third Generation

16. **Hannah Woodbury** (Joseph, Daniel) was born on 21 Jan 1876 in Whiteford Center, Monroe County, Michigan, USA. She died on 17 Apr 1946 in Toledo, Lucas County, Ohio, USA. She was buried in Sylvania, Lucas County, Ohio, USA.

Hannah married **William Charles Bell** son of William Charles Bell Sr and Sarah Ann Merryfield on 11 Jan 1893 in Lucas Co., Ohio. William was born in May 1872 in Michigan. He died on 27 Apr 1935 in Toledo, Lucas County, Ohio, USA. He was buried in Sylvania, Lucas County, Ohio, USA.

They had the following children:

    57 F   i. **Brazel B Bell** was born on 5 Mar 1902 in Ottawa Lake, Monroe County, Michigan, USA. She died on 11 Mar 1941 in Toledo, Lucas County, Ohio, USA. She was buried in Sylvania, Lucas County, Ohio, USA.
               Brazel married **Joe C Wearer** on 24 Nov 1919 in Detroit, Michigan, USA. Joe was born about 1898 in Pennsylvania.

+   58 M   ii. **Lawson R Bell** was born on 27 Feb 1896. He died on 25 Jul 1971.

20. **Mary Jane Woodbury** (Joseph, Daniel) was born on 10 Feb 1863 in Michigan, United States. She died on 6 Jan 1888.

Mary married **Robert W. Lovewell** son of Charles Lovewell and Sarah Adelaide Noble on 4 Dec 1881 in Whiteford township, Monroe County, Michigan. Robert was born in 1859 in Whiteford township, Monroe County, Michigan.

They had the following children:

    59 M   i. **George Orrin Lovewell** was born in 1887 in Springfield, Ohio.

    60 F   ii. **Jennie M Lovewell** was born in 1882.

21. **Henry Harrison Woodbury** (Joseph, Daniel) was born in May 1861 in Michigan, USA. He died on 1 Nov 1935 in Flint, Genesee, Michigan.

Henry married **Elizabeth Poland** in 1886. Elizabeth was born in Dec 1871 in Ohio.

They had the following children:

    61 F   i. **Ella Woodbury** was born in Aug 1888 in Michigan.

    62 M   ii. **Joseph A. Woodbury** was born on 3 Apr 1887 in Petersburg, Monroe, Michigan, USA. He died on 19 Jan 1954. He was buried in Flint, Genesee County, Michigan, USA.

23. **Lucille (Madeline) Woodbury** (Joseph, Daniel) was born on 21 Feb 1869 in Petersburg,
Michigan. She died on 17 Dec 1948 in Toledo, Lucas Co., Ohio.

Lucille married **Charles C Harwald** on 26 Feb 1895 in Whiteford, Monroe Co., Michigan. Charles was born about 1870 in Ottawa Lake, Monroe Co., Michigan. He died on 14 Jul 1945 in Toledo, Lucas Co., Ohio.

They had the following children:

+   63 F   i.   **Dorothy M. Harwald** was born about 1902.

24. **Julius Woodbury** (Joseph, Daniel) was born in Sep 1868 in Michigan. He died on 24 Jan 1956 in Riga, Lenawee, Michigan, USA.

Julius married (1) **Mary E Colton** daughter of Isaac Colton and Jennie Boudrie on 4 Sep 1893 in Whiteford, Monroe, Michigan, USA. Mary was born on 22 Oct 1873 in Monroe, Michigan. She died on 4 Feb 1936 in Riga, Lenawee, Michigan, USA.

They had the following children:

    64 F   i.   **Goldie Woodbury** was born on 16 Jul 1894 in Whiteford, Monroe, Michigan, USA. She died on 24 Dec 1986 in Sylvania, Lucas County, Ohio, USA. She was buried on 27 Dec 1986 in Riga, Lenawee, Michigan, USA.
Goldie married **John H Fritz Jr** son of John J. Fritz and Caroline C "Carrie" Rodesiler on 13 Nov 1912 in Lucas County, Ohio, United States. John was born on 15 Jun 1886 in Riga, Lenawee, Michigan, United States. He died on 16 Sep 1974 in Adrian, Lenawee, Michigan, United States.

    65 F   ii.   **Mable M. Woodbury** was born on 29 Mar 1896 in Michigan.

    66 M   iii.   **Gordon C Woodbury** was born about 1902 in Michigan.

Julius married (2) **Louise Cousino** daughter of William Cousino and Julia Reno on 20 Oct 1938 in Erie, Monroe, Michigan, USA. Louise was born in Nov 1882 in Michigan.

26. **George Elmer Woodbury** (Lyman, Daniel) was born on 17 Sep 1871 in Michigan. He died on 7 Apr 1946 in Monroe, Monroe, Michigan, USA.

George married **Emma Susan Wade** daughter of John Wade and Cathrine Wade on 26 Oct 1892 in Whiteford, Monroe, Michigan, United States. Emma was born on 7 Nov 1873 in Michigan. She died on 5 Feb 1958 in Monroe, Monroe, Michigan, USA.

They had the following children:

    67 F   i.   **Irene Elberta Woodbury** was born on 28 Jul 1893 in Michigan.

She died in Feb 1979 in Dundee, Michigan.

> 68 F   ii. **Ethel Woodbury** was born in Oct 1899 in Michigan. She died on 18 Jul 1974 in Parkview Hospital-Toledo, Ohio.

27. **Maggie A Woodbury** (Lyman, Daniel) was born about 1874 in Michigan.

Maggie married **William J Poley** son of George Poley and Hennora Shudy on 4 Oct 1895 in Sylvania, Ohio, USA. William was born about 1861 in Ohio.

They had the following children:

+   69 F   i. **Bernice E Poley** was born on 6 May 1895. She died on 15 Jan 1987.

29. **Ella M. Woodbury** (Lyman, Daniel) was born in Dec 1864 in Michigan. She died on 3 May 1902 in Olivet, Eaton, Michigan, United States.

Ella married **George Robert Harrington** son of William Anson Harrington and Alma Louisa Daily about 1886. George was born on 8 Nov 1859 in Columbia, Lorain, OH. He died on 9 May 1930 in Bellevue, Eaton, Michigan, USA.

They had the following children:

> 70 F   i. **Pearl Pauline Harrington** was born on 20 Aug 1887 in Walton, Eaton, Michigan. She died on 28 Jun 1953 in Lansing, Ingham, Michigan, United States.

30. **Addie Cordelia Woodbury** (Lyman, Daniel) was born about 1866 in Monroe County, Michigan, USA.

Addie married **Charles Mitchell** . Charles was born in Cincinnati, Ohio, USA.

They had the following children:

> 71 M   i. **George Forest Mitchell** was born on 10 Jun 1889 in Monroe County, Michigan, USA. He died on 23 Dec 1962.

31. **Harvey Woodbury** (Albert Joseph, Daniel) was born on 12 Apr 1859 in Whiteford, Monroe, Michigan, USA. He died on 27 Dec 1943 in Toledo, Lucas, Ohio, USA. He was buried in Toledo, Lucas County, Ohio, USA.

Harvey married **Catherine Schmidt** daughter of John Schmidt and Mary Schmidt on 17 Apr 1888 in Toledo, Lucas, Ohio, USA. Catherine was born on 11 Aug 1864 in Germany. She died on 9 Nov 1928 in Toledo, Lucas County, Ohio, USA. She was buried in Toledo, Lucas County, Ohio, USA.

They had the following children:

> 72 M   i. **Arthur Joseph Woodbury** was born on 28 Oct 1888 in Toledo, Lucas County, Ohio, USA. He died on 7 Oct 1918 in Toledo, Lucas

County, Ohio, USA. He was buried in Toledo, Lucas County, Ohio, USA.

| 73 M | ii. | **Clarence Woodbury** was born on 27 Jun 1903. |

73 M   ii.   **Clarence Woodbury** was born on 27 Jun 1903.

74 M   iii.   **James Woodbury** was born in 1904.

75 F   iv.   **Ruth Woodbury** was born in 1910.

76 M   v.   **Julius D Woodbury** was born on 15 Dec 1899.

77 M   vi.   **Lambert Woodbury** was born on 10 May 1893 in Ohio.

78 F   vii.   **Nettie Woodbury** was born on 7 Aug 1891. She died on 3 Apr 1966 in Mercy Hospital, Toledo, Lucas, Ohio.

79 F   viii.   **Helen Woodbury** was born on 25 Apr 1898.

80 M   ix.   **Harvey Peter Woodbury** was born on 23 Apr 1895 in Toledo, Lucas County, Ohio, USA. He died on 30 Jul 1986 in Toledo, Lucas County, Ohio, USA. He was buried in Ottawa Hills Cem. Harvey married **Minnie** .

34. **Sarah Ann Woodbury** (Albert Joseph, Daniel) was born on 15 Nov 1857. She died on 10 Oct 1916 in Toledo, Lucas, Ohio, USA.

Sarah married (1) **Fred H Krieger** on 7 Apr 1871 in Lucas County, Ohio, USA. Fred was born about 1850 in Germany. He died before 1912.

They had the following children:

81 M   i.   **Harvey Krieger** was born about 1884.

82 M   ii.   **James Krieger** was born about 1883 in Toledo, Lucas, Ohio, USA.

83 F   iii.   **Sarah Krieger** was born on 15 Aug 1877.

84 F   iv.   **Emma Krieger** was born about 1880 in Toledo, Lucas, Ohio, USA.

85 F   v.   **Martha Krieger** was born in 1888 in Toledo, Ohio. She died on 8 Dec 1959 in Toledo, Lucas, Ohio.

86 F   vi.   **Amelia Frances Krieger** was born on 28 Feb 1892 in Toledo, Lucas, Ohio, USA.

87 M   vii.   **Charles A. Krieger** was born on 4 Jul 1881 in Toledo, Lucas, Ohio, USA.

Sarah married (2) **John Thompson** son of Abraham Thompson and Mary McCoy on 5 Oct 1912 in Toledo, Ohio. John was born in 1856 in Indiana.

36. **Martha Jane WOODBURY** (Albert Joseph, Daniel) was born on 18 Jun 1847 in Whiteford, Monroe, Michigan, USA. She died on 20 Apr 1932 in Lucas, Ohio, United States.

Martha married **Henry Hugh Herr** . Henry was born about 1848 in Michigan. He died in Ohio.

Henry and Martha had the following children:

    88 M   i. **Henry Herr** was born about 1870 in Ohio.

+   89 F   ii. **Elizabeth Alida Herr** was born on 12 Aug 1876. She died on 8 Apr 1948.

43. **Benjamin Franklin Noble** (Anna Woodbury, Daniel) was born on 4 Sep 1839 in Ravenna, Portage, Ohio, USA. He died about 1915 in , , Michigan, USA.

Benjamin married (1) **Viola Robideaux** daughter of Peter Robideaux and Polly Pugnette on 25 Apr 1871 in Monroe, Michigan, USA. Viola was born on 12 Sep 1850 in Michigan, USA. She died on 8 Feb 1910 in Whiteford, Monroe, Michigan, USA. She was buried on 10 Feb 1910.

They had the following children:

    90 F   i. **Maud Noble** was born in Jul 1878 in Whiteford Center, Monroe, Michigan, USA. She died on 4 Sep 1962 in Bedford, Monroe, Michigan.

    91 M   ii. **George Noble** was born in Jul 1878 in Whiteford, Monroe, Michigan. He died in Whiteford, Monroe, Michigan, USA.

    92 F   iii. **Della Noble** was born about 1874 in Michigan USA.

    93 F   iv. **Berthia Noble** was born about 1872 in Michigan USA.

    94 F   v. **Doris Noble** was born in Aug 1890 in Whiteford, Monroe, Michigan.

    95 M   vi. **Frank Noble** was born on 3 Jan 1880 in Whiteford, Monroe, Michigan USA. He died on 26 Jul 1941 in Rfd Temperance, Monroe, Michigan, USA. He was buried in Lambertville, Monroe County, Michigan, USA.
Frank married **Loretta A** . Loretta was born in 1889 in Ohio.

    96 F   vii. **Loretta Anna Noble** was born on 5 Jan 1889 in Erie, Monroe, Michigan, United States. She died on 10 Jul 1977 in Punta Gorda, Charlotte, Florida, USA.

    97 M   viii. **Clarence Charles Noble** was born on 12 Feb 1870 in Monroe, Monroe, Michigan, USA. He died on 22 Nov 1933 in MARTINS

FERRY, BELMONT COUNTY, OHIO. He was buried in Nov 1933 in BOWERSTON CEMETERY, BOWERSTON, HARRISON COUNTY, OHIO.

      98 M   ix. **Charles H Noble** was born in 1871 in Whiteford, Monroe, Michigan. He died on 6 Mar 1928 in Kalamazoo, Kalamazoo, Michigan. He was buried in Cooper, Kalamazoo County, Michigan, USA.

Benjamin married (2) **Cerol** in 1870 in Monrroe County, Mi. Cerol was born in 1851.

50. **Matilda Woodbury** (David, Daniel) was born in 1848 in Geauga, Ohio, United States. She died on 1 Jan 1908 in Toledo, Lucas, Ohio, United States.

Matilda married **John Ferris** son of Samuel W Ferris and Margaret Ferris on 29 May 1862. John was born in Dec 1835 in Ohio.

They had the following children:

      99 M   i. **Frank Earnest Ferris** was born in Mar 1870 in Michigan. He died on 7 Jan 1947 in Ypsilanti, Washtenaw County, Michigan, USA. He was buried in Royal Oak, Oakland County, Michigan, USA.

     100 F   ii. **Clara M Ferris** was born in 1873 in Michigan.

+   101 F   iii. **Ella Mae Ferris** was born on 17 May 1879. She died on 22 Oct 1933.

     102 M   iv. **George Ferris** was born in Michigan.

51. **Martha Woodbury** (David, Daniel) was born on 4 Nov 1846 in Blissfield, Michigan, USA. She died on 23 Sep 1906 in Whiteford, Monroe, Michigan, USA. She was buried in Whiteford Union Cemetery, Lambertville, Monroe Co., MI.

Martha married **Dominic Gee** in Michigan, USA. Dominic was born on 10 Mar 1849 in Toledo, Lucas, Ohio, United States. He died on 4 Feb 1904 in Whiteford, Monroe, Michigan, USA. He was buried in Whiteford Union Cemetery, Lambertville, Monroe Co., MI.

They had the following children:

+   103 F   i. **Ida Mae Gee** was born on 6 Jun 1887. She died on 14 Jan 1960.

+   104 M   ii. **Levi Alexander Gee** was born on 13 Sep 1882. He died on 24 Aug 1963.

     105 M   iii. **William Gee** was born on 13 Aug 1873. He died on 13 Feb 1935.

     106 F   iv. **Sarah Gee** was born on 22 Feb 1872 in Michigan. She died on 8

Jul 1960.

Sarah married **George Bookey** after 1887. George was born in Jul 1870 in New York, USA. He died on 1 Jul 1960 in Toledo, Lucas, Ohio, USA. He was buried in Whiteford Union Cemetery, Lambertville, Monroe Co., MI.

+ 107 F v. **Mary Ann Gee** was born on 18 Aug 1873. She died on 27 Dec 1947.

+ 108 F vi. **Ella C Gee** was born on 5 Jul 1880. She died on 22 May 1970.

   109 M vii. **Willis Gee** was born about 1875 in Michigan.

52. **John Milton Woodbury** (David, Daniel) was born on 27 Sep 1870 in Blissfield, Michigan, USA. He died on 11 Feb 1943 in Toledo, Ohio, USA. He was buried in Toledo Memorial Cemetary.

John married **Anna Eliza Cornwill** daughter of Russell Cornwill and Florence Philinda Austin on 5 Jun 1891 in Palmyria, Michigan, USA. Anna was born on 15 Sep 1875 in

Palmyria, Lenawee, Michigan, United States. She died on 19 Feb 1958 in Toledo, Ohio, USA. She was buried in Roselawn Cem. Monroe, Mi.

They had the following children:

   110 F i. **Annabelle Woodbury** was born in 1913 in Sylvania, Lucas County, Ohio, United States of America. She died on 22 Oct 1918 in Toledo, Lucas County, Ohio, United States of America.

+ 111 F ii. **Luella Bell Woodbury** was born on 18 Jun 1910. She died on 5 Oct 1996.

+ 112 F iii. **Laura Louise Woodbury** was born on 19 Aug 1916. She died on 31 Aug 1989.

+ 113 M iv. **Charles Leon Woodbury Sr** was born on 28 Feb 1899. He died on 3 Dec 1985.

+ 114 F v. **Nola Mae Woodbury** was born on 23 Aug 1919. She died on 17 Apr 1990.

+ 115 M vi. **Cecil Allen Woodbury Sr** was born on 4 Mar 1907. He died on 26 Jun 1976.

+ 116 F vii. **Maude Florence Woodbury** was born on 12 Aug 1894. She died on 7 Jul 1977.

+ 117 M viii. **Herman Roy Woodbury** was born on 23 Apr 1892. He died on 4 Feb 1975.

+ 118 M ix. **Harry Fay Woodbury Sr.** was born on 9 Dec 1896. He died on 25 Dec 1981.

+ 119 F x. **Iva Irene May Queen Woodbury** was born on 5 Oct 1905. She died on 14 Jul 1980.

120 M xi. **Loyal Woodbury** was born on 24 Dec 1901 in Lennawee, Michigan, USA. He died on 23 Apr 1903 in Monroe, Michigan, USA.

53. **Edwin Bowers** (Polly S Woodbury, Daniel) was born in Jun 1842 in Ohio, USA. He died on 12 Dec 1922 in Wood County, Ohio. He was buried in Dec 1922 in Walbridge, Wood County, Ohio, USA.

Edwin married **Mary Jane Chandler** daughter of John C. Chandler and Mary Long on 4 Mar 1890 in Toledo, Lucas, Ohio, USA. Mary was born on 4 Mar 1864 in Genoa, Ottawa, Ohio, USA. She died on 27 Jun 1917 in Wood County, Ohio, USA. She was buried in Jun 1917 in Walbridge, Wood County, Ohio, USA.

They had the following children:

121 F i. **Cinderella Bowers** was born on 1 Jul 1886 in Allen Township, Ottawa, Ohio, USA. She died on 14 Jul 1952 in Toledo, Lucas, Ohio, USA. She was buried on 17 Jul 1952 in Walbridge, Wood, Ohio, USA.

122 M ii. **James Edwin Bowers** was born on 14 May 1900 in Lake Township, Wood, Ohio, USA. He died on 7 Jun 1968 in Toledo, Lucas, Ohio, United States.

Fourth Generation

58. **Lawson R Bell** (Hannah Woodbury, Joseph, Daniel) was born on 27 Feb 1896 in Michigan, United States of America. He died on 25 Jul 1971.

Lawson married **Esther** . Esther was born about 1898 in Ohio.

They had the following children:

123 F i. **Margaret J Bell**

63. **Dorothy M. Harwald** (Lucille (Madeline) Woodbury, Joseph, Daniel) was born about 1902 in Michigan.

Dorothy married (1) **James Stretchbery** son of Charles Frederick "Fred" Stretchbery and Effie Bell Miller. James was born on 12 Mar 1898 in Weston, Wood, Ohio, USA. He died on 10 Dec 1986 in Saint Petersburg, Pinellas, Florida, USA.

She had the following children:

124 M   i. **James Stretchbery**

69. **Bernice E Poley** (Maggie A Woodbury, Lyman, Daniel) was born on 6 May 1895 in South Bend, St Joseph, IN, USA. She died on 15 Jan 1987 in South Bend, St Joseph, Indiana, United States of America.

Bernice married **Ray W Jackson** on 27 Sep 1913 in St. Joseph, Indiana. Ray was born on 1 Aug 1894 in Indiana,United States of America. He died on 25 Dec 1920 in South Bend, Indiana.

They had the following children:

     125 M   i. **John A Jackson** was born on 12 Nov 1916 in South Bend, St Joseph, IN, USA. He died on 3 Jan 1969 in South Bend, St Joseph, IN, USA.

     126 F   ii. **Joyce A Jackson**

     127 F   iii. **Virginia M Jackson**

89. **Elizabeth Alida Herr** (Martha Jane WOODBURY, Albert Joseph, Daniel) was born on 12 Aug 1876 in Toledo, Lucas Co., Ohio. She died on 8 Apr 1948 in Toledo, Lucas Co., Ohio. She was buried in Waterville, Lucas, Ohio, USA.

Elizabeth married **Anthony S. Yount** son of George Washington Yount and Saphronia Cobley in 1893. Anthony was born on 19 Apr 1872 in Waterville, Lucas, Ohio, USA. He died on 3 Aug 1919 in Toledo, Lucas, Ohio, USA. He was buried on 5 Aug 1919 in Waterville, Lucas, Ohio, USA.

Anthony and Elizabeth had the following children:

     128 F   i. **Ethel Mae Yount** was born on 22 Jan 1895 in Toledo, Lucas, Ohio, USA. She died on 17 Jul 1943 in Toledo, Lucas, Ohio, USA.

+   129 F   ii. **Bertha Martha Yount** was born on 22 Feb 1902. She died on 24 Feb 1983.

     130 M   iii. **Ernest Roy Yount** was born on 24 May 1896 in Toledo, Lucas, Ohio, USA. He died on 26 Feb 1983 in Burbank, Los Angeles, California, USA. He was buried in Los Angeles, Los Angeles, California, USA.

     131 M   iv. **Clarence Albert Yount** was born on 17 Mar 1901 in Toledo, Lucas, Ohio, USA. He died on 19 Jul 1940 in Los Angeles County, California, USA. He was buried in Glendale, Los Angeles, California, USA.

     132 M   v. **Henry Charles Yount** was born on 24 Jul 1898 in Toledo, Lucas, Ohio USA. He died on 17 Nov 1924 in Toledo, Lucas, Ohio, USA. He was buried on 20 Nov 1924 in Waterville, Lucas, Ohio, USA.

101. **Ella Mae Ferris** (Matilda Woodbury, David, Daniel) was born on 17 May 1879 in Michigan. She died on 22 Oct 1933 in Adrian, Michigan. She was buried in Adrian, Lenawee County, Michigan, USA.

Ella married **Orry Joel Westgate** on 18 Nov 1913 in Adrian, Michigan. Orry was born on 27 May 1873 in Raisin Twp, Lenawee Co.. He died on 20 Jul 1947 in United Brethern Church Adrian MI. He was buried in Adrian, Lenawee County, Michigan, USA.

They had the following children:

133 F	i.	**Elda L Westgate** was born on 9 Sep 1915 in Adrian, Michigan. She died on 24 Jun 1974 in Adrian, Michigan.
134 M	ii.	**Maynard J Westgate** was born on 17 Nov 1904 in Adrian, Michigan. He died on 18 Oct 1983 in Adrian, Lenawee, Michigan, United States of America.
+ 135 M	iii.	**Ferris Nelson Westgate** was born on 20 Sep 1916. He died on 24 Jun 1973.

103. **Ida Mae Gee** (Martha Woodbury, David, Daniel) was born on 6 Jun 1887 in Whiteford, Monroe, Michigan, United States. She died on 14 Jan 1960 in Windsor, 1654297, Ontario, Canada. She was buried on 17 Jan 1970 in LaSalle Township Ceme. LaSalle, MI.

Ida married (1) **William Emmanuel Gautz** on 16 Mar 1904 in East Raisinville Church, Monroe, MI. William was born on 24 Jul 1878 in LaSalle, MI. He died on 26 Oct 1943 in Monroe, MI. He was buried in LaSalle Township Ceme, LaSalle, MI.

They had the following children:

+ 136 M	i.	**Lloyd William Gautz** was born on 5 Mar 1905. He died on 1 Apr 1970.
+ 137 M	ii.	**Henry George Gautz** was born on 18 Dec 1908. He died on 4 Nov 1969.
138 F	iii.	**Grace Ida Gautz** was born on 16 Jun 1920 in Monroe, Monroe, Michigan, USA. She died on 5 Sep 2008 in Monroe, Monroe, Michigan, USA. Grace married **Chester Dewain Brost** on 11 Sep 1941 in Ida, MI. Chester was born on 20 Jun 1917 in Monroe, MI. He died on 9 May 2009 in Monroe, MI.
139 F	iv.	**Olga Loretta Gautz** was born on 21 Jul 1917 in Monroe, MI. She died on 27 Feb 1984 in St. Charles Hosp. Toledo, OH. She was buried in Chestnut Grove Ceme., Bradner, OH.
+ 140 F	v.	**Gertrude Mary Gautz** was born on 16 Feb 1911. She died on 18

Feb 1992.

+   141 M   vi.   **Clarence David Gautz** was born on 5 May 1922. He died on 27
                   Jan 1985.

    142 M   vii. **Baby Boy Gautz** was born on 8 Aug 1925. He died on 8 Aug
                   1925.

    143 F   viii. **Edna Mae Gautz** was born on 17 Sep 1914 in Strasburg, MI. She
                   died on 9 Jun 1973 in Mercy Hosp. Monroe, MI. She was buried on
                   12 Jun 1973 in Roselawn Mem. Cemetary, LaSalle, MI.

    144 M   ix.   **Earl Chester Gautz** was born on 8 May 1907 in Strausberg, MI.
                   He died on 26 Jan 1994 in Monroe, MI. He was buried in Roselawn
                   Memorial Park Ceme. LaSalle, MI.

Ida married (2) **Elmer Everett McKibbon** on 15 May 1946. Elmer was born on 14
Mar 1894 in Cleveland, OH.

104. **Levi Alexander Gee** (Martha Woodbury, David, Daniel) was born on 13 Sep 1882
     in Center, Emmet, Michigan, United States. He died on 24 Aug 1963 in Toledo,
     Lucas, Ohio, United States. He was buried in Whiteford Union Cemetery,
     Lambertville, Monroe Co., MI.

     Levi married (1) **Olive L. Rice** after 1897. Olive was born on 7 May 1882 in
     Richfield Center, Ohio. She died on 7 Apr 1977 in Toledo, Lucas, Ohio, USA. She
     was buried in Whiteford Union Cemetery, Lambertville, Monroe Co., MI.

     They had the following children:

     145 F   i.   **Ruth Gee** was born after 1897.

     146 F   ii.   **Frances Gee** was born after 1897.

     147 M   iii. **Robert W. Gee** was born on 3 Jan 1916 in Ohio, USA. He died on
                   3 May 2001 in Deerfield, Lenawee Co., Michigan, USA. He was
                   buried in Whiteford Union Cemetery, Lambertville, Monroe Co., MI.

     Levi married (2) **Ruby S. Friess** on 26 Nov 1913 in 1913 Clayton, Genesee, MI.
     Ruby was born in Nov 1894 in Monroe Co., Michigan, USA. She died on 26 May
     1918 in LaSalle,

     LaSalle Co., MI. She was buried on 28 May 1918 in Whiteford Union Cemetery,
     Lambertville, Monroe Co., MI.

107. **Mary Ann Gee** (Martha Woodbury, David, Daniel) was born on 18 Aug 1873 in
     Michigan. She died on 27 Dec 1947 in Toledo, Lucas, Ohio, United States.

     Mary married **James B. Cousino** in 1897. James was born on 29 Apr 1878. He died on 12 Sep 1952 in Summerfield, Monroe, Michigan, USA.

They had the following children:

+ 148 M   i. **Frank G Cousino** was born on 27 Oct 1909. He died on 1 Jun 1971.

   149 F   ii. **Beulah Cousino**

   150 M   iii. **James Radist Cousino** was born on 25 Jan 1903 in Lasalle, Monroe, Michigan, USA. He died on 28 Jun 1989 in Sylvania, Lucas, Ohio, USA.

   151 F   iv. **Frieda Cousins** was born in 1899 in , , Michigan, USA. Frieda married **Mack Morse** on 19 Apr 1915 in Monroe, Michigan, USA. Mack was born about 1894 in Michigan.

+ 152 M   v. **Arnold Joseph COUSINO** was born on 3 Jul 1905. He died on 15 Mar 1962.

   153 M   vi. **Ernest Cousino** was born on 1 Jun 1936. He died in Mar 1987.

108. **Ella C Gee** (Martha Woodbury, David, Daniel) was born on 5 Jul 1880 in Michigan. She died on 22 May 1970 in Monroe, Monroe, Michigan, United States of America. She was buried on 25 May 1970 in Roselawn Memorial Park Ceme. LaSalle, MI.

Ella married **Delbert Couture** on 19 Oct 1903 in LaSalle Township, MI. Delbert was born on 24 Mar 1880 in LaSalle Township, MI. He died on 25 Aug 1961. He was buried on 28 Aug 1961 in Roselawn Memorial Park Ceme. LaSalle, MI.

They had the following children:

   154 F   i. **Sarah Couture** was born on 10 May 1917 in Michigan. She died on 8 Dec 2003 in Monroe, Monroe, Michigan, United States.

   155 F   ii. **Lucy Couture** was born about 1905 in Michigan. She died in 1983 in Monroe, Monroe, Michigan.

   156 M   iii. **Edward Couture** was born on 15 Jan 1916 in Michigan. He died on 24 Feb 1997 in Monroe, Monroe, Michigan, United States.

+ 157 F   iv. **Ruby Couture** was born about 1915. She died on 16 Nov 2006.

   158 F   v. **Lillian Couture** was born after 1903.

   159 F   vi. **Edith Couture** was born in 1903.

111. **Luella Bell Woodbury** (John Milton, David, Daniel) was born on 18 Jun 1910 in Monroe, Michigan, USA. She died on 5 Oct 1996 in Toledo, Ohio, USA.

Luella married **Elroy Bud Hinds** son of Hartley White Hinds and Florence Jessie Long. Elroy was born on 30 Apr 1907 in Toledo, Lucas, Ohio, USA. He died on 3 Nov 1961 in Toledo, Lucas, Ohio.

They had the following children:

+   160 F   i. **Charmayne Hinds** .

112. **Laura Louise Woodbury** (John Milton, David, Daniel) was born on 19 Aug 1916 in Toledo, Lucas, Ohio, USA. She died on 31 Aug 1989 in Naples, Collier, Florida, USA. She was buried in Cremated.

Laura married **Hartley Wilbur Hinds** son of Hartley White Hinds and Florence Jessie Long on 22 Jul 1933 in Monroe, Michigan, USA. Hartley was born on 24 Feb 1916 in Toledo, Lucas, Ohio, USA. He died on 20 May 1985 in Naples, Collier, Florida, USA. He was buried in Cremated.

They had the following children:

+   161 M   i. **Jimmy Alan Hinds** was born on 26 Feb 1947. He died on 27 Jun 2001.

+   162 M   ii. **Tommy Gene Hinds** was born on 20 May 1944. He died on 29 May 2005.

+   163 F   iii. **Kathleen Ann Hinds**

+   164 M   iv. **Hartley William Hinds**

   165 M   v. **Keith Ray Hinds** was born on 12 Feb 1952 in Toledo, Lucas, Ohio, USA. He died on 26 Aug 2011 in Naples, Collier, Florida. Keith married **Recinda Joy Kennison** on 6 Oct 1990 in Collier, Florida.

   166 F   vi. **Anna Marie Hinds** was born on 15 Sep 1942 in Toledo, Lucas, Ohio, USA. She died on 28 Dec 1943 in Toledo, Lucas, Ohio, United States.

+   167 F   vii. **Nancy Jean Hinds** was born on 8 May 1936. She died on 28 Mar 1988.

+   168 F   viii. **Patsy Louise Hinds** was born on 4 Oct 1934. She died on 19 Oct 2006.

+   169 M   ix. **Jerry Eugene Hinds** was born on 24 Mar 1938. He died on 15 Sep 2005.

+   170 F   x. **Sandra Sue Hinds**

+   171 M   xi. **Richard Leroy Hinds** was born on 23 Aug 1939. He died on 23 Mar 1998.

113. **Charles Leon Woodbury Sr** (John Milton, David, Daniel) was born on 28 Feb 1899 in Lennawee, Michigan, USA. He died on 3 Dec 1985 in Platka, Florida, USA. He was buried in 1984 in Palatka, Putnam, Florida, USA.

Charles married **Iva Rosette Duty** daughter of Wesley Daniel Duty and June Orella Struble on 17 May 1924 in , Monroe, Michigan, USA. Iva was born on 18 May 1908 in Carson City, Montcalm, Michigan, USA. She died on 14 Apr 1960 in , , Florida, USA. She was buried in Jun 1964 in Palatka, Putnam, Florida, USA.

They had the following children:

	172 M	i.	**Daniel J. Woodbury** was born on 18 Dec 1934. He died on 18 Dec 1934 in Forest, Missaukee, Michigan, USA.
	173 F	ii.	**Carol Woodbury**
+	174 M	iii.	**Ralph Woodbury**
	175 M	iv.	**Rollin J. Woodbury** was born on 3 Oct 1936 in , , Michigan, USA. He died on 3 Oct 1936.
	176 F	v.	**June Orella Woodbury** was born on 24 Jan 1923 in Monroe, Michigan. She died on 28 Jul 2006 in Titusville, Brevard, Florida, USA.
	177 M	vi.	**Clarence Charles "Butch" Woodbury Jr** was born on 30 Apr 1925 in Monroe Monro, Michigan. He died on 9 Aug 2006 in Lambertville, Monroe, Michigan, USA. He was buried in Lambertville, Monroe County, Michigan, USA. Clarence married **Caroline** .
	178 M	vii.	**Howard Woodbury** was born on 2 Feb 1929 in Michigan, USA. Howard married **Etta Marie Holton** on 5 Jul 1947 in Charlotte, Eaton, Michigan, USA. Etta was born about 1930 in Jackson, Michigan.
	179 F	viii.	**Gladys Woodbury**

114. **Nola Mae Woodbury** (John Milton, David, Daniel) was born on 23 Aug 1919 in Monroe, Michigan, USA. She died on 17 Apr 1990 in Bowling Green, Ohio, USA.

Nola married **Edward J Rahm** son of Edward Rahm and Elizabeth Christina Young on 5 Sep 1934. Edward was born on 15 May 1912 in Sherman, Wisconsin. He died on 20 Feb 1972 in Fort Myers, Lee, Florida, USA.

They had the following children:

+	180 F	i.	**Dianna Mae Rahm**

+ 181 F   ii. **Judy Ann Rahm** was born on 14 Apr 1941. She died on 28 Jun 1988.

+ 182 M   iii. **Edward J. Rahm II** was born on 2 Feb 1938. He died on 4 Aug 1997.

115. **Cecil Allen Woodbury Sr** (John Milton, David, Daniel) was born on 4 Mar 1907 in Lennawee County, MI. He died on 26 Jun 1976. He was buried in Ottawa Hills, Lucas
County, Ohio, USA.

Cecil married **Ida Isabelle Long** daughter of William Allen Long and Hulda Amelia Wescott on 13 Oct 1933. Ida was born on 10 May 1917 in Ohio, United States. She died on 31 Jan 1978 in Toledo, Lucas, Ohio, United States of America. She was buried in Ottawa Hills, Lucas County, Ohio, USA.

They had the following children:

+ 183 M   i. **Cecil Allen Woodbury Jr.** was born on 2 Oct 1935. He died on 12 Dec 2015.

+ 184 F   ii. **Edith Woodbury**

116. **Maude Florence Woodbury** (John Milton, David, Daniel) was born on 12 Aug 1894 in Lennawee, Michigan, USA. She died on 7 Jul 1977 in Labelle, Hendry, Florida, USA. She was buried in Denaud, Hendry County, Florida, USA.

Maude married (1) **Louis Shanaway** son of Louis Francois Shanaway and Marie Judith Angelique Kane in 1916. Louis was born on 15 Apr 1888 in Illinois, United States. He died on 27 Jan 1924 in Monroe, Monroe, Michigan, USA. He was buried in Monroe, Monroe County, Michigan, USA.

They had the following children:

   185 M   i. **Jesse J. Shanaway** was born on 1 Sep 1924 in Monroe, Monroe, Michigan, USA. He died on 15 Jan 1946

+ 186 M   ii. **Louis Leander Shanaway** was born on 1 Jul 1920. He died on 3 Dec 1982.

+ 187 F   iii. **Mary Ann Shanaway** was born on 2 Aug 1917. She died on 18 Aug 2002.

Maude married (2) **William Green** . William was born about 1875 in Illinois. He died in 1958.

Maude married (3) **Aaron Auten** .

They had the following children:

188 M   iv. **Harry Auten** .

189 M   v. **Gerald Auten** .

117. **Herman Roy Woodbury** (John Milton, David, Daniel) was born on 23 Apr 1892 in Lennawee County, MI. He died on 4 Feb 1975 in Cocoa Beach, Brevard, FL.

Herman married (1) **Emma Shanaway** daughter of Louis Francois Shanaway and Marie Judith Angelique Kane on 6 Aug 1910 in Monroe, MI. Emma was born on 8 Nov 1890 in IL. She died on 28 Dec 1926.

Herman and Emma had the following children:

190 F   i. **Opal Woodbury**

191 F   ii. **Edith A. Woodbury** was born on 24 Mar 1916 in Toledo, Lucas Co., OH. She died on 17 May 1916 in Toledo, Lucas Co., OH.

\+   192 M   iii. **John Louis Woodbury** was born on 4 Apr 1913. He died on 15 Jan 1992.

\+   193 M   iv. **Herman William Woodbury Jr Jr.** was born on 9 Jun 1917. He died on 24 Mar 1940.

Herman married (2) **Ruth Elsie Suffell** . Ruth was born on 5 Nov 1898 in Germany. She died on 3 Feb 1984 in Rockledge, Brevard, Florida, USA.

118. **Harry Fay Woodbury Sr.** (John Milton, David, Daniel) was born on 9 Dec 1896 in Tecumseh, Michigan. He died on 25 Dec 1981 in Monroe, Michigan, USA. He was buried in La Salle, Monroe County, Michigan, USA.

Harry married **Alice Marie Bosenbark** daughter of Irving Bosenbark and Anna Bertha Cornell on 2 Sep 1920 in Detroit, Michigan, USA. Alice was born on 2 Nov 1903 in , Monroe, Michigan, USA. She died on 11 Jan 1996 in Monroe, Monroe, Michigan, United States of America.

They had the following children:

\+   194 M   i. **Ralph William Woodbury** was born on 8 Oct 1928. He died on 16 Apr 1986.

\+   195 M   ii. **Raymond O. Woodbury**

196 M   iii. **Norman E. Woodbury** .

\+   197 M   iv. **Harry Fay Woodbury Jr.** was born on 6 Sep 1921. He died on 1 Apr 1981.

119. **Iva Irene May Queen Woodbury** (John Milton, David, Daniel) was born on 5 Oct 1905 in Lennawee, Michigan, USA. She died on 14 Jul 1980 in Toledo, Lucas, Ohio, United States.

Iva married (1) **Red Houck** on 21 Sep 1922 in Monroe, Monroe, Michigan, USA. Red was born about 1902 in Pennsylvania.

They had the following children:

+   198 F   i.   **Dorothy Houck** was born in 1923. She died in Nov 1984.

Iva married (2) **Zenith Sherman Osenbaugh** son of Charles A Osenbaugh and Ida Mae Parker about 1925. Zenith was born on 24 Oct 1906 in Blanchard, Putnam, Ohio. He died on 1 May 1966 in Toledo,Ohio.

Zenith and Iva had the following children:

+   199 F   ii.   **Marlene Mae Osenbaugh** was born in Sep 1939. She died on 27 Nov 2003.

+   200 F   iii.   **Beverly Jean Osenbaugh** was born on 16 Jan 1937. She died on 26 Nov 1994.

     201 F   iv.   **Sharon Osenbaugh** .

+   202 F   v.   **Ruth Osenbaugh**

     203 M   vi.   **Sherman Osenbaugh** was born in 1938 in Toledo, Lucas, Ohio, United States. He died on 5 Dec 1939 in Toledo, Lucas, Ohio, USA.

+   204 F   vii.   **Annabelle Osenbaugh** was born in Feb 1929. She died on 20 Nov 2013.

+   205 M   viii.   **Tommie Milton Ray Osenbaugh** was born on 16 Sep 1927. He died on 30 Jun 2012.

+   206 M   ix.   **Zenith Charles Osenbaugh "Babe"** was born on 26 May 1925. He died on 7 Jun 1999.

+   207 F   x.   **Bonnie Osenbaugh**

+   208 F   xi.   **Joyce Marie Osenbaugh** was born on 15 Jun 1934. She died on 27 Nov 2003.

Iva married (3) **Arthur Snyder** .

They had the following children:

+   209 M   xii. **Arthur John Snyder** .

Iva married (4) **James Edington** .

She had the following children:

+   210 M   xiii. **Alvin L. Woodbury** was born on 15 Jan 1922. He died on 8 Dec
             2007.

Fifth Generation

129. **Bertha Martha Yount** (Elizabeth Alida Herr, Martha Jane WOODBURY, Albert
     Joseph, Daniel) was born on 22 Feb 1902 in Toledo, Lucas, Ohio, USA. She died
     on 24 Feb 1983 in Garden Grove, Orange, California, USA. She was buried in
     Santa Ana, Orange County, California, USA.

     Bertha married **Charles Ivo Brown** son of Richard Oliver Brown and Clara
     Cramer about 1924 in Ohio, USA. Charles was born on 17 Jan 1893 in Benton
     Ridge, Hancock, Ohio, USA. He died on 22 Aug 1953 in Genoa, Ottawa, Ohio,
     USA. He was buried in , Hancock, Ohio, USA.

     They had the following children:

+   211 M   i. **Gerald Leroy Brown** was born on 5 Aug 1926. He died on 10 Jun
             1983.

135. **Ferris Nelson Westgate** (Ella Mae Ferris, Matilda Woodbury, David, Daniel) was
     born on 20 Sep 1916 in Adrian, Lenawee, Michigan, United States. He died on 24
     Jun 1973 in Adrian, Lenawee, Michigan, United States.

     Ferris married **Clarice Marie Thompson** on 24 Jul 1937 in Adrian, Michigan.
     Clarice was born on 2 Jun 1920 in Adrian, Lenawee, Michigan, United States. She
     died on 10 Feb 2002 in Adrian, Lenawee, Michigan, United States.

     They had the following children:

     212 F   i. **Sherrill J Westgate**
                 Sherrill married **Tony F Webb** on 20 Apr 1981 in San Diego,
                 California, USA.

     213 M   ii. **Private** .

136. **Lloyd William Gautz** (Ida Mae Gee, Martha Woodbury, David, Daniel) was born
     on 5 Mar 1905 in Monroe, MI. He died on 1 Apr 1970 in Lake City, MI. He was
     buried on 4 Apr 1970 in Stittsville Ceme. Missaukee County, MI.

     Lloyd married **Hyla Maye Battenfield** .

     They had the following children:

214 M   i. **John Walter Gautz** .
John married **Tara Ann Walsh** .

215 M   ii. **James Lee Gautz** .
James married **Tina Marie Hand** .

216 M   iii. **Lloyd William Gautz** .
Lloyd married **Barbara Pryzyski** .

217 F   iv. **Ida Maye Gautz** .
Ida married **Thomas Duane Myers** .

218 F   v. **Esther Marie Gautz** .
Esther married **James Douglass Burress** .

137. **Henry George Gautz** (Ida Mae Gee, Martha Woodbury, David, Daniel) was born on 18 Dec 1908 in Strausburg, MI. He died on 4 Nov 1969 in Monroe, MI. He was buried on 7 Nov 1969 in Roselawn Memorial Park Ceme. LaSalle, MI.

Henry married **Ethel A. Havekost** on 20 Aug 1932 in Zion Lutheran Parsonage, Monroe, MI. Ethel was born on 21 Mar 1911 in Michigan, USA. She died on 7 Jun 2003 in Monroe, Monroe, Michigan, USA. She was buried in Lasalle, Monroe, Michigan, USA.

They had the following children:

219 F   i. **Arnette Irma Gautz** .

220 F   ii. **Baby Girl Gautz** was born on 29 Jun 1936. She died on 29 Jun 1936. She was buried in Zion Luth. Ceme., Monroe, MI.

221 M   iii. **Stanley Edward Gautz** was born on 29 Mar 1938 in Monroe, MI. He died on 27 Mar 2014 in Toledo, Lucas, Ohio.

140. **Gertrude Mary Gautz** (Ida Mae Gee, Martha Woodbury, David, Daniel) was born on 16 Feb 1911 in Strausburg, MI. She died on 18 Feb 1992 in Frenchtown Nursing Home, Monroe, MI. She was buried in Roselawn Memorial Park, LaSalle, Mi.

Gertrude married **Camillus C. Soleau** . Camillus was born on 6 Jan 1907 in Michigan, USA. He died on 5 Sep 1991 in Monroe, Monroe, Michigan, USA.

They had the following children:

222 M   i. **Henry Lawrence Soleau** was born on 9 Oct 1935 in Monroe, MI. He died on 15 Oct 1951 in Blissfield, MI. He was buried in Roselawn Memorial Park Cemetery, LaSalle, MI.

223 M   ii. **Clarence William Soleau** was born in 1932 in Monroe, MI. He died in 1994 in Monroe, MI. He was buried on 14 Feb 1994 in

Roselawn Memorial Park Cemetery, LaSalle, MI.

141. **Clarence David Gautz** (Ida Mae Gee, Martha Woodbury, David, Daniel) was born on 5 May 1922 in LaSalle, MI. He died on 27 Jan 1985 in St Vincent's Hosp., Toledo, OH. He was buried in Lasalle, Monroe, Michigan, USA.

Clarence married (1) **Mary Alice Whitcomb** daughter of Charles Edwin Whitcomb and Amy Swart on 4 Jun 1950 in Erie, Monroe, Michigan, USA. Mary was born on 4 Sep 1921 in Toledo, Lucas, Ohio, USA. She died on 20 Jun 1993 in Erie, Monroe, Michigan, USA. She

was buried in Lasalle, Monroe, Michigan, USA.

They had the following children:

> 224 F   i.   **Donna Jean Gautz**
>
> 225 M   ii.   **David William Gautz**
>
> 226 F   iii.   **Ruth Ann Gautz**
>
> 227 F   iv.   **Suzan Gautz** was born on 24 Oct 1961 in Lasalle, Monroe, Michigan, USA. She died on 24 Oct 1961 in Lasalle, Monroe, Michigan, USA. She was buried in Lasalle, Monroe, Michigan, USA.
>
> 228 F   v.   **Amy Louise Gautz**
> Amy married **Bossie** .

Clarence married (2) **Donna Marie Ellison** .

They had the following children:

> +   229 M   vi.   **Daniel Wayne Gautz** .

148. **Frank G Cousino** (Mary Ann Gee, Martha Woodbury, David, Daniel) was born on 27 Oct 1909 in Bedford, Monroe, Michigan. He died on 1 Jun 1971 in 4357 Samaria Rd, Temperance, MI. He was buried on 13 Jan 1971 in Whiteford Union Cemetary, Whiteford, MI.

Frank married **Edna Austin March** on 11 Jan 1941 in Sylvania, OH.

They had the following children:

> 230 F   i.   **Ellen Cousino** .
> Ellen married **Armbrust** .

152. **Arnold Joseph COUSINO** (Mary Ann Gee, Martha Woodbury, David, Daniel) was born on 3 Jul 1905 in Erie, Monroe, Michigan, USA. He died on 15 Mar 1962 in Petersburg, Monroe, Michigan, USA. He was buried in Erie, Monroe County, Michigan, USA.

Arnold married (1) **Irma B Cousino** . Irma was born about 1908 in Michigan.

Arnold married (2) **Elizabeth Anna Baum** on 2 Feb 1924 in , Monroe, Michigan, USA. Elizabeth was born on 11 Feb 1908 in Stockbridge, Ingham, Michigan, United States. She died in 1982 in Petersburg, Michigan, USA. She was buried on 24 May 1982 in Lambertville, Monroe County, Michigan, USA.

They had the following children:

+   231 F   i. **Ellen Marie Cousino** was born on 29 Apr 1926. She died on 10 Jan 1997.

157. **Ruby Couture** (Ella C Gee, Martha Woodbury, David, Daniel) was born about 1915 in Michigan. She died on 16 Nov 2006 in Monroe, Monroe, MI.

Ruby married **Arnold Ansul** .

They had the following children:

232 F   i. **Joan Ella Ansul** .

160. **Charmayne Hinds** (Luella Bell Woodbury, John Milton, David, Daniel).

Charmayne married **Donald Gochenour** .

They had the following children:

233 M   i. **Jon Donald Gochenour**

234 M   ii. **Jay Robert Gochenour** .

+   235 F   iii. **Jennifer Ann Gochenour** .

236 M   iv. **Jeffrey Allen Gochenour** .

161. **Jimmy Alan Hinds** (Laura Louise Woodbury, John Milton, David, Daniel) was born on 26 Feb 1947 in Toledo, Lucas, Ohio, United States. He died on 27 Jun 2001 in Toledo, Lucas, Ohio, United States of America.

Jimmy married **Patricia Hall** daughter of Melvin Morral Hall and Betty Lorraine Flanders.

They had the following children:

+   237 F   i. **Anna Marie Hinds**

+   238 F   ii. **Evelyn Hinds**

+   239 M   iii. **Jimmy Hinds Jr**

162. **Tommy Gene Hinds** (Laura Louise Woodbury, John Milton, David, Daniel) was born on 20 May 1944 in Toledo, Lucas, Ohio, USA. He died on 29 May 2005 in Durant, Hillsborough, Florida.

Tommy married (1) **Grace Beatrice Eckhart** daughter of Ollie Gerald Eckhart and Loretta Mae Nigh in Jan 1962. Grace died in Oct 2005.

They had the following children:

+   240 F   i.   **Debbie Sue Hinds**

       241 M   ii.   **Larry Douglass Hinds**

+   242 F   iii.   **Loretta Mae Hinds** was born on 31 Jan 1963. She died on 16 Feb 1985.

Tommy married (2) **Bonnie Lee Reilly** daughter of Robert Elmer Reilly and Mary Yvonne on 7 Jan 1972. Bonnie was born on 6 Jan 1948 in Paterson, Passaic, New Jersey, USA. She died on 18 Mar 2016.

They had the following children:

+   243 F   iv.   **Marjorie Ann Hinds**

+   244 F   v.   **Mary Hinds**

+   245 M   vi.   **Tommy Gene Hinds**

+   246 F   vii.   **Marie Elaine Hinds**

Tommy married (3) **Anna Mae Hardy** daughter of Charles Robert Hardy and Virginia May South.

They had the following children:

+   247 F   viii.   **Diana Hinds**

+   248 M   ix.   **Joe Ray Hinds**

+   249 F   x.   **Terrie L Hinds**

+   250 M   xi.   **Tommy Gene Hinds**

+   251 F   xii.   **Karrie Lynn Hinds**

Tommy married (4) **Donna** . Donna was born in 1962. She died in 2008.

They had the following children:

+ 252 M xiii. **Richard Mannon**

+ 253 M xiv. **Donald Mannon**

+ 254 F xv. **Cynthia Mannon**

163. **Kathleen Ann Hinds** (Laura Louise Woodbury, John Milton, David, Daniel) was born in Toledo, Lucas, Ohio, USA.

Kathleen married (1) **James Clark Culbreath 1** son of Julian Pervus Culbreath and Maida Lorel Bickford. James was born on 20 Aug 1940 in Fort Myers, Lee, Florida. He died on 23 Sep 1996 in Bradenton, Manatee, Florida. He was buried in Bradenton, Manatee County, Florida, USA.

They had the following children:

+ 255 M i. **James Samuel Culbreath**

+ 256 M ii. **Merton Daniel Culbreath**

+ 257 M iii. **Timothy Alan Culbreath**

+ 258 F iv. **Laura Lorel Culbreath**

Kathleen married (2) **Randy Bibbee** .

164. **Hartley William Hinds** (Laura Louise Woodbury, John Milton, David, Daniel) was born in Toledo, Lucas, Ohio, USA.

Hartley married **Georgette** .

They had the following children:

259 F i. **Michelle Danielle Hinds** .

260 F ii. **Christine Hinds** .

261 F iii. **Hartley William Hinds Jr** .

167. **Nancy Jean Hinds** (Laura Louise Woodbury, John Milton, David, Daniel) was born on 8 May 1936 in Toledo, Lucas, Ohio, USA. She died on 28 Mar 1988 in Jefferson, Kentucky.

Nancy married **Freeman Lloyd Coats** son of Dempsey Otho Coats and Easter Aldora on 29 Jan 1953 in Monroe, Michigan, USA. Freeman was born on 9 Mar 1927. He died on 27 Mar 1985 in Louisville, Jefferson, Kentucky, USA.

They had the following children:

+   262 F   i. **Mary Evelyn Coats**

+   263 M   ii. **Vincent Ray Coats**

+   264 M   iii. **James Eric Coats**

+   265 F   iv. **Karen Fay Coats**

+   266 F   v. **Donna Jean Coats**

+   267 M   vi. **Freeman Lloyd Coats**

168. **Patsy Louise Hinds** (Laura Louise Woodbury, John Milton, David, Daniel) was born on 4 Oct 1934 in Toledo, Lucas, Ohio, USA. She died on 19 Oct 2006 in Frostproof, Polk, Florida, USA.

Patsy married (1) **Paul Morris** . Paul was born on 1 Feb 1932 in Toledo, Lucas, Ohio, USA. He died in 2009.

They had the following children:

+   268 F   i. **Debra Sue Morris**

+   269 F   ii. **Pamela Louise Morris**

+   270 M   iii. **Paul Sonny Morris**

Patsy married (2) **Robert Lee McKinney** in 1967 in Hendry County, Florida. Robert was born on 4 Jan 1931. He died on 23 Mar 2013.

They had the following children:

    271 M   iv. **Mark McKinney**

+   272 M   v. **Robert McKinney**

+   273 M   vi. **Ricky Eugene Mckinney**

Patsy married (3) **Carl Lockwood** .

169. **Jerry Eugene Hinds** (Laura Louise Woodbury, John Milton, David, Daniel) was born on 24 Mar 1938 in Toledo, Lucas, Ohio, USA. He died on 15 Sep 2005 in Frostproof, Polk, Florida.

Jerry married **Shirley Jean Eckhart** daughter of Ollie Gerald Eckhart and Loretta Mae Nigh about 1960.

They had the following children:

+   274 F   i. **Sherry Hinds**

275 M   ii. **Jerry Eugene Hinds Jr Jr**
Jerry married **Carol Jean Myers** on 15 Sep 1988 in Collier, Florida.

170. **Sandra Sue Hinds** (Laura Louise Woodbury, John Milton, David, Daniel) was born in Toledo, Lucas, Ohio, USA.

Sandra married (1) **Dale Earton Lyon** son of Earle Zenas Lyon and Ethel Levina Switser in Jan 1959. Dale was born in St Johnsbury, Caledonia, Vermont, USA.

They had the following children:

+   276 F   i. **Wanda Kay Lyon**

+   277 M   ii. **Randall Kelvin Lyon**

+   278 M   iii. **Donald Ray Lyon**

Sandra married (2) **James Mansel Kurtz** son of Theodore D Kurtz and Shirley Ellen Morris on 15 Apr 1977 in Naples, Collier, Florida, USA.

They had the following children:

279 F   iv. **Jami Sue Kurtz** was born in Naples, Collier, Florida, USA.

171. **Richard Leroy Hinds** (Laura Louise Woodbury, John Milton, David, Daniel) was born on 23 Aug 1939 in Toledo, Lucas, Ohio, USA. He died on 23 Mar 1998 in Piedmont, Calhoun, Alabama, United States of America,.

Richard married **Shelby Pierce** daughter of Pierce in Jul 1957 in Collier, Florida.

They had the following children:

+   280 M   i. **Richard Hinds Jr**

+   281 F   ii. **Phyllis Hinds** .

174. **Ralph Woodbury** (Charles Leon, John Milton, David, Daniel) was born in Monroe, Michigan, USA.

Ralph married **Marcille Shank** on 26 Feb 1949.

They had the following children:

282 F   i. **Cindy Sue Woodbury**
Cindy married **Paul Garland** .

283 F   ii. **Peggy Marcille Woodbury**

Peggy married **Rusty Lee Smith** on 7 Sep 1988.

| 284 M | iii. | **Michael Doyle Woodbury** |

| 285 F | iv. | **Vicky Lynn Woodbury** |

Vicky married **Dennis Dale La Point** on 6 Jun 1969.

| 286 M | v. | **Ralph William Woodbury**. |

Ralph married **Debra Deer** .

180. **Dianna Mae Rahm** (Nola Mae Woodbury, John Milton, David, Daniel)

Dianna married (1) **Jerry Henry McCauslin** in Jan 1969 in Lee, Florida

Dianna married (2) **Allen J. Parker** on 6 Feb 1996.

They had the following children:

| 287 M | i. | **Allen Johnson Parker** |

181. **Judy Ann Rahm** (Nola Mae Woodbury, John Milton, David, Daniel) was born on 14 Apr 1941 in Toledo, Lucas, Ohio, USA. She died on 28 Jun 1988 in Toledo, Lucas, Ohio, USA.

Judy married **Muriel Rogers** .

Muriel and Judy had the following children:

| 288 F | i. | **Vicky Lynn Rogers** . |

| 289 F | ii. | **Dawn Michelle Rogers** . |

+ | 290 F | iii. | **Christina Marie Rogers** |

| 291 F | iv. | **Cheryl Lynn Rogers** |

182. **Edward J. Rahm II** (Nola Mae Woodbury, John Milton, David, Daniel) was born on 2 Feb 1938 in Trilby Lucas, Ohio. He died on 4 Aug 1997. He was buried in Luckey, Wood County, Ohio, USA.

Edward married (1) **Pat Kothe** .

They had the following children:

| 292 M | i. | **Edward Rahm III** |

+ | 293 F | ii. | **Luann Marie Rahm** |

Edward married (2) **Marlene Jewell** on 31 Dec 1991 in Holland, Ohio.

183. **Cecil Allen Woodbury Jr.** (Cecil Allen, John Milton, David, Daniel) was born on 2 Oct 1935 in Lucas County, Ohio, United States. He died on 12 Dec 2015 in New York, USA. He was buried in La Salle, Monroe County, Michigan, USA.

Cecil married **Delores Duty** . Delores was born on 19 Dec 1937 in Michigan. She died on 12 Oct 2012 in New York. She was buried in La Salle, Monroe County, Michigan, USA.

They had the following children:

    294 M   i. **Don Woodbury** .

184. **Edith Woodbury** (Cecil Allen, John Milton, David, Daniel) was born about 1934 in Ohio. She was buried in Ottawa Hills, Lucas County, Ohio, USA.

Edith married **Dale W Musser** . Dale was born in 1932. He was buried in Ottawa Hills, Lucas County, Ohio, USA.

They had the following children:

\+   295 M   i. **Larry D. Musser** .

\+   296 M   ii. **Gary D. Musser**

\+   297 M   iii. **Dale A. Musser** .

\+   298 M   iv. **Robert E. Musser**

186. **Louis Leander Shanaway** (Maude Florence Woodbury, John Milton, David, Daniel) was born on 1 Jul 1920 in Monroe, Monroe, Michigan, United States. He died on 3 Dec 1982 in Alva, Lee, Florida, USA. He was buried in Gotha, Orange County, Florida, USA.

Louis married **Barbara Mary Stuard** on 15 Aug 1941 in Wood, Ohio, United States. Barbara was born on 23 Aug 1923 in Frankfort, Clinton, Indiana, United States. She died on 15 Jan 1982 in Orlando, Orange, Florida, United States of America.

They had the following children:

\+   299 M   i. **Larry Michael Shanaway.**

\+   300 M   ii. **Dennis Paul Shanaway** .

\+   301 F   iii. **Leanne Marie Shanaway** .

\+   302 F   iv. **Karen Lynn Shanaway** .

\+   303 M   v. **James Marvin Shanaway**

\+   304 F   vi. **Barbara Jean Shanaway** was born on 29 Mar 1942. She died on

4 Mar 1996.

+   305 M   vii.   **David Louis Shanaway** was born on 30 May 1947. He died on 9 Jan 1995.

187. **Mary Ann Shanaway** (Maude Florence Woodbury, John Milton, David, Daniel) was born on 2 Aug 1917 in Monroe, Monroe, Michigan, USA. She died on 18 Aug 2002 in Toledo, Lucas, Ohio, USA.

Mary married **Ernest Wagner** on 13 Apr 1935 in Lake City, Benzie, Michigan, USA.

They had the following children:

  306 M   i.   **Francis Eugene Wagner**
              Francis married **Victoria Simon** on 10 Dec 1985.

  307 M   ii.   **Jesse William Wagner**
              Jesse married **Jenny Skrine** on 11 May 1983.

  308 F   iii.   **Donna Lou Wagner** was born on 22 Jan 1936. She died on 5 Jun 1937.

  309 F   iv.   **Carolyn Mae Wagner**
              Carolyn married **James Spas** in 1954.

192. **John Louis Woodbury** (Herman Roy, John Milton, David, Daniel) was born on 4 Apr 1913 in Monroe, Michigan, USA. He died on 15 Jan 1992 in Cocoa, FL.

John married **Corine Anna Monroe** daughter of Charles Monroe and Louise Lozen on 14 Apr 1934 in Toledo, Lucas, Ohio, USA. Corine was born on 29 Jun 1918 in Toledo, Lucas, Ohio, USA. She died on 25 Sep 1994 in Cocoa, Brevard, FL.

John and Corine had the following children:

+   310 F   i.   **Luann Ruth Woodbury** was born on 26 Jul 1943. She died on 22 Jan 2001.

  311 F   ii.   **Elsie Louise Woodbury** was born in 1941 in Toledo, Lucas, Ohio, USA. She died in 1941.

+   312 M   iii.   **Jimmie Allen Woodbury**

+   313 M   iv.   **Ronald Gene Woodbury**

+   314 M   v.   **William Ray Woodbury** was born on 29 Mar 1936. He died on 27 Oct 1994.

+   315 M   vi.   **Jack Leroy Woodbury**

316 M   vii.   **Walter Lenord Woodbury** was born in 1940 in Toledo, Lucas, Ohio, USA. He died in 1940.

317 M   viii.   **Jerry George Woodbury** was born on 2 Apr 1939 in Toledo, Lucas, Ohio, USA. He died on 23 Sep 1948.

193. **Herman William Woodbury Jr Jr.** (Herman Roy, John Milton, David, Daniel) was born on 9 Jun 1917 in Monroe, Monroe Co., MI. He died on 24 Mar 1940 in Toledo, Lucas Co., OH. He was buried in Toledo, Lucas County, Ohio, USA.

Herman married **Wilma Marguerite Fox** . Wilma was born on 20 Jun 1919 in Toledo, Lucas County, Ohio, USA. She died on 12 Nov 1997 in Oregon, Lucas County, Ohio, USA. She was buried in Toledo, Lucas County, Ohio, USA.

They had the following children:

+   318 F   i.   **Darlene Joyce Woodbury**

194. **Ralph William Woodbury** (Harry Fay, John Milton, David, Daniel) was born on 8 Oct 1928 in , Monroe, Michigan, USA. He died on 16 Apr 1986.

Ralph married **Donna Mae Sype** on 31 Jan 1953. Donna was born on 2 Sep 1930. She died on 13 Sep 2009.

They had the following children:

319 F   i.   **Ralph William Woodbury**

+   320 F   ii.   **Loretta Kay Woodbury**

195. **Raymond O. Woodbury** (Harry Fay, John Milton, David, Daniel)

Raymond married **Jo Ann Complo** on 3 Nov 1951 in Monroe, Monroe, Michigan, USA.

Raymond and Jo had the following children:

321 M   i.   **Timothy Woodbury** .

322 F   ii.   **Susan Woodbury** .

+   323 M   iii.   **Thomas R. Woodbury** .

197. **Harry Fay Woodbury Jr.** (Harry Fay, John Milton, David, Daniel) was born on 6 Sep 1921 in Monroe MI. He died on 1 Apr 1981 in Monroe MI. He was buried in La Salle, Monroe County, Michigan, USA.

Harry married **Mary Alice Bert** . Mary died on 29 Jan 2008. She was buried in La Salle, Monroe County, Michigan, USA.

They had the following children:

+   324 M   i. **Daniel W. Woodbury**

198. **Dorothy Houck** (Iva Irene May Queen Woodbury, John Milton, David, Daniel) was born in 1923. She died in Nov 1984.

Dorothy married **Richard Beaty "Red"** son of Reb Beaty and Lillian M Wyant. Richard was born on 17 Aug 1922 in West Virginia, United States. He died on 17 Dec 1986 in Toledo, Lucas, Ohio, USA.

They had the following children:

   325 F   i. **Peggy Beaty** .
           Peggy married **Mike Miller** .

   326 M   ii. **Carl Beaty** .
           Carl married **Patricia** .

   327 M   iii. **Richard Beaty** .
           Richard married **Danielle** .

   328 M   iv. **Terry Beaty** .
           Terry married **Donna** .

+   329 M   v. **Robert Beaty** .

   330 F   vi. **Delilah Beaty** .

   331 M   vii. **Larry Beaty** died in Mar 1968.

+   332 M   viii. **Roland Beaty** was born on 5 Feb 1944. He died on 29 Mar 2007.

199. **Marlene Mae Osenbaugh** (Iva Irene May Queen Woodbury, John Milton, David, Daniel) was born in Sep 1939 in Washington, Lucas Co., OH, USA. She died on 27 Nov 2003 in
Toledo, Lucas Co., OH, USA.

Marlene married **Crowder** .

They had the following children:

   333 M   i. **Bobby Crowder** .

   334 F   ii. **Sarah Crowder** .

   335 F   iii. **Cheryl Crowder** .

   336 F   iv. **Luann Crowder** .

337 M   v. **Charles Crowder** .

338 M   vi. **Kenneth Knapp Crowder** .

200. **Beverly Jean Osenbaugh** (Iva Irene May Queen Woodbury, John Milton, David, Daniel) was born on 16 Jan 1937 in Toledo Lucas, Ohio. She died on 26 Nov 1994. She was buried in Perrysburg, Wood County, Ohio, USA.

Beverly married **Herbert William Slater** son of William Henry Slater Jr and Hazel Slater. Herbert was born on 26 Aug 1928 in Perrysburg, Wood County, Ohio, USA. He died on 15 Feb 1981 in Toledo, Lucas County, Ohio, USA. He was buried in Perrysburg, Wood County, Ohio, USA.

They had the following children:

339 M   i. **Charles E. Slater** .
         Charles married **Shirley Mae** .

202. **Ruth Osenbaugh** (Iva Irene May Queen Woodbury, John Milton, David, Daniel) was born about 1931 in Toledo, Lucas, Ohio, USA. She died in Toledo, Lucas, Ohio, USA.

Ruth married **Harry James Rogers** son of Harry James ROGERS and Hazel May HINDS on 19 Feb 1951 in Monroe, Monroe, Michigan, USA. Harry was born on 25 May 1928 in Toledo, Lucas County, Ohio. He died on 4 Oct 1977 in Alpena, Alpena, Michigan, USA. He was buried on 6 Oct 1977 in Wilson Twp., Alpena Co., Michigan.

They had the following children:

340 F   i. **Donna Rogers** .

341 M   ii. **Michael Rogers** .

342 M   iii. **Gary Rogers** .

343 F   iv. **Vicky Rogers** .

204. **Annabelle Osenbaugh** (Iva Irene May Queen Woodbury, John Milton, David, Daniel) was born in Feb 1929 in Toledo, Lucas, OH, USA. She died on 20 Nov 2013 in Missaukee Co., MI, USA. She was buried in Lake City, Missaukee County, Michigan, USA.

Annabelle married **Lewis Loyd "Lewie" Knapp** son of Theodore Knapp and Vesta Viola Bedo on 21 Feb 1948 in Lake City, Missaukee, Michigan, USA. Lewis was born on 12 Apr 1911 in Michigan, USA. He died on 11 Jul 1995 in Lake City, Missaukee County, Michigan, USA. He was buried in Lake City, Missaukee County, Michigan, USA.

They had the following children:

344   i. **Marcella Map Knapp** was born in Missaukee Co., MI, USA. Marcella died on 19 Sep 1958 in Star City, Missaukee Co., MI, USA. Marcella was buried in Lake City, Missaukee County, Michigan, USA.

345 M   ii. **Private** .

205. **Tommie Milton Ray Osenbaugh** (Iva Irene May Queen Woodbury, John Milton, David, Daniel) was born on 16 Sep 1927 in Ohio. He died on 30 Jun 2012 in Zephyrhills, Florida.

Tommie married (1) **Mary** .

They had the following children:

346 F   i. **Janet Osenbaugh** .

347 F   ii. **Jackie Osenbaugh** .

348 F iii. **Kathy Osenbaugh** .

349 F iv. **Sheila Osenbaugh** .

350 F   v. **Debbie Osenbaugh** .

Tommie married (2) **Jacquelyn Catherine DuShane** daughter of Myron Joseph "Pippi" DuShane and Ada Mae (Mimi) Aubry. Jacquelyn was born on 22 Jul 1928 in Toledo, Lucas, Ohio, United States. She died on 5 Jun 1997 in Toledo, Lucas, Ohio, United States.

They had the following children:

+   351 M vi. **Bernard Aubry Du Shane** was born on 4 Nov 1947. He died on 14 Jan 1988.

206. **Zenith Charles Osenbaugh "Babe"** (Iva Irene May Queen Woodbury, John Milton, David, Daniel) was born on 26 May 1925 in Toledo, Lucas, Ohio, United States. He died on 7 Jun 1999. He was buried in OH.

He had the following children:

352 M   i. **John Osenbaugh** .

353 M ii. **Howard Osenbaugh** .

354 F iii. **Dorothy Jean Osenbaugh** .

355 F iv. **Sharon Osenbaugh** .

356 F   v. **Linda Osenbaugh** .

357 F   vi. **Anna Osenbaugh** .

358 F   vii. **Mary Osenbaugh** .

Zenith married (2) **Dorothy** .

Zenith married (3) **Vivian Mae Birch "Dink"** on 25 Mar 1972 in Lee, Florida.

Zenith married (4) **Judith Pratt** .

They had the following children:

+   359 M   viii. **Harry Osenbaugh** .

    360 M   ix. **Cecil Osenbaugh Jr.** .

    361 M   x. **Frank Sherman Osenbaugh** .

+   362 F   xi. **Judy Elaine Osenbaugh** .

+   363 M   xii. **Robert Wayne Osenbaugh** .

207. **Bonnie Osenbaugh** (Iva Irene May Queen Woodbury, John Milton, David, Daniel) was born in Ohio.

Bonnie married **James Brown** .

They had the following children:

+   364 F   i. **Lori Brown** .

+   365 F   ii. **Jeanna Brown** .

    366 F   iii. **Nadaja Brown** .
        Nadaja married **Charles Bondy** .

+   367 F   iv. **Bonita Brown** .

208. **Joyce Marie Osenbaugh** (Iva Irene May Queen Woodbury, John Milton, David, Daniel) was born on 15 Jun 1934 in Toledo, Ohio. She died on 27 Nov 2003.

Joyce married (1) **Pete Starkey** .

They had the following children:

    368 F   i. **Terry Starkey** .

369 F   ii. **Joanne Starkey** .

Joyce married (2) **Don Swicegood** .

They had the following children:

370 M   iii. **Shawn Swicegood** .

371 F   iv. **Karen Swicegood** .

Joyce married (3) **Carl Sargent** .

They had the following children:

372 M   v. **Todd Allen Sargent** .

373 F   vi. **Tanya Sargent** .

209. **Arthur John Snyder** (Iva Irene May Queen Woodbury, John Milton, David, Daniel).

Arthur married **Virginia** .

They had the following children:

374 M   i. **John Snyder Jr.** .

375 M   ii. **Darren Snyder** .

376 F   iii. **Joyce Snyder** .

377 F   iv. **Judy Snyder** .

210. **Alvin L. Woodbury** (Iva Irene May Queen Woodbury, John Milton, David, Daniel) was born on 15 Jan 1922. He died on 8 Dec 2007 in Apopka, Orange, Florida, United States of America.

Alvin married **Millie** .

They had the following children:

378 M   i. **Joseph Leroy Woodbury** .

379 M   ii. **Darrel Anthony Woodbury** .

+   380 M   iii. **David A. Woodbury** .

Sixth Generation

211. **Gerald Leroy Brown** (Bertha Martha Yount, Elizabeth Alida Herr, Martha Jane WOODBURY, Albert Joseph, Daniel) was born on 5 Aug 1926 in Toledo, Lucas, Ohio, USA. He died on 10 Jun 1983 in Scottsdale, Maricopa, Arizona, USA. He was buried in Phoenix, Maricopa County, Arizona, USA.

Gerald married **Margueritte Jeanne Carr** . Margueritte was born on 5 Dec 1925 in Metamora, Fulton, Ohio, USA. She died on 3 Oct 2005 in Oregon, Lucas, Ohio, USA.

They had the following children:

    381 F   i. **Krispy Brown** .
                  Krispy married (1) **Snyder** .
                  Krispy married (2) **Ian William Holter** son of Ian D Holter and Norma Titus on 26 Mar 1995 in Clark, Nevada. Ian was born on 8 Oct 1962 in Berwick, Columbia, Pennsylvania, USA. He died on 23 Oct 2004 in Bowling Green, Warren, Kentucky, USA.

    382 M   ii. **Jeffery Brown** He died in 1983.

229. **Daniel Wayne Gautz** (Clarence David Gautz, Ida Mae Gee, Martha Woodbury, David, Daniel).

Daniel married **Dianne Rose Godlewski** .

They had the following children:

    383 F   i. **Denise Angella Gautz**

    384 F   ii. **Deborah Nicole Gautz**

    385 M   iii. **Daniel Richard Gautz**

    386 F   iv. **Dawn Michelle Gautz**

231. **Ellen Marie Cousino** (Arnold Joseph COUSINO, Mary Ann Gee, Martha Woodbury, David, Daniel) was born on 29 Apr 1926 in Toledo, Lucas, Ohio, USA. She died on 10 Jan 1997 in Toledo, Lucas, Ohio, USA. She was buried in Jan 1997 in Lambertville, Monroe County, Michigan, USA.

Ellen married (1) **Harold Richard McClure** . Harold was born on 5 Jul 1918. He died on 5 Jun 1986 in Homosassa, Citrus, Florida, USA. He was buried in Jun 1986 in Lambertville, Monroe County, Michigan, USA.

They had the following children:

    387 M   i. **David Lee McClure**

    388 M   ii. **Charles William McClure**

| 389 F | iii. | **Sandra Ellen McClure** |

| 390 M | iv. | **William Thomas McClure** was born on 20 Mar 1963 in Toledo, Lucas, Ohio, United States. He died on 14 Aug 2015 in Jefferson Parish, Louisiana, USA. |

| 391 F | v. | **Kathryn Ann McClure** was born on 5 Mar 1954 in Toledo, Lucas, Ohio, USA. She died on 16 Jan 1955. She was buried in Lambertville, Monroe County, Michigan, USA. |

| 392 M | vi. | **Buddy Richard McClure** was born on 19 Dec 1949 in Ohio, United States. He died on 8 Jan 2007 in Ohio. He was buried in Walbridge, Wood County, Ohio, USA. |

| 393 M | vii. | **Warren Tolly McClure** was born on 20 Mar 1963 in Toledo, Lucas, Ohio, United States. He died on 22 Feb 2011 in Cincinnati, Hamilton, Ohio. |

She had the following children:

| 394 F | viii. | **Joyce Elizabeth Cousino** |

| 395 M | ix. | **Robert Raymond Cousino** |

| 396 M | x. | **Mitchell Arnold Cousino** was born on 25 Feb 1945 in Stockbridge, Ingham, Michigan, USA. He died on 7 Apr 2015. |

235. **Jennifer Ann Gochenour** (Charmayne Hinds, Luella Bell Woodbury, John Milton, David, Daniel).

Jennifer married **Douglas Finch** .

They had the following children:

| 397 F | i. | **Kaleigh Ashton Finch** . |

237. **Anna Marie Hinds** (Jimmy Alan Hinds, Laura Louise Woodbury, John Milton, David, Daniel)

Anna married **Derrick Harris** .

They had the following children:

| 398 F | i. | **Dakoda Marie Harris** |

| 399 M | ii. | **William Allen Harris** |

238. **Evelyn Hinds** (Jimmy Alan Hinds, Laura Louise Woodbury, John Milton, David, Daniel)

Evelyn married **Derrick Johnson** .

They had the following children:

    400 F   i. **Erica Johnson** .

    401 F   ii. **Jackie Hinds** .

    402 M   iii. **Devontay Johnson** .

    403 F   iv. **Dedra Johnson** .

    404 M   v. **Derrion Johnson** .

239. **Jimmy Hinds Jr** (Jimmy Alan Hinds, Laura Louise Woodbury, John Milton, David, Daniel)

Jimmy married **Wendy** .

They had the following children:

    405 M   i. **Jeremy Hinds** .

    406 M   ii. **Alex Hinds** .

    407 M   iii. **Sam Hinds** .

240. **Debbie Sue Hinds** (Tommy Gene Hinds, Laura Louise Woodbury, John Milton, David, Daniel) was born in Los Angeles, California.

Debbie and **Jerry Leroy Cass** had the following child:

+   408 M   i. **Jessie Daniel Cass**

Debbie married (2) **Richard Dane Scott** son of Robert William Scott and Elayne Fae Campbell. Richard was born in Bay Village, Cuyahoga, Ohio, United States.

242. **Loretta Mae Hinds** (Tommy Gene Hinds, Laura Louise Woodbury, John Milton, David, Daniel) was born on 31 Jan 1963. She died on 16 Feb 1985.

Loretta married **Dennis James Cass** on 19 Sep 1981 in Clark, Nevada.

They had the following children:

    409 F   i. **Barbara Ann Cass** .

    410 M   ii. **Dennis Cass** .

243. **Marjorie Ann Hinds** (Tommy Gene Hinds, Laura Louise Woodbury, John Milton, David, Daniel)

Marjorie married (1) **John Scott** .

She had the following children:

+   411 F   i.   **Brittany Lee Hinds**

244. **Mary Hinds** (Tommy Gene Hinds, Laura Louise Woodbury, John Milton, David, Daniel)

She had the following children:

     412 M   i.   **Michael Borowski**

+   413 F   ii.   **Samantha Roberts**

245. **Tommy Gene Hinds** (Tommy Gene Hinds, Laura Louise Woodbury, John Milton, David, Daniel)

He had the following children:

     414 F   i.   **Nicole Richmond** .

246. **Marie Elaine Hinds** (Tommy Gene Hinds, Laura Louise Woodbury, John Milton, David, Daniel)

She had the following children:

     415 F   i.   **Myah Rose Hinds**

     416 M   ii.   **Travis Andrew Priestly**

247. **Diana Hinds** (Tommy Gene Hinds, Laura Louise Woodbury, John Milton, David, Daniel)

Diana married **Joseph Norman Vardaman**

They had the following children:

     417 M   i.   **Andrew Joseph Vardaman**

     418 F   ii.   **Roseanna Marlene Vardaman**

+   419 F   iii.   **Shawna Marie Vardaman**

     420 M   iv.   **Garold Joseph Vardaman**

     421 M   v.   **Justin Joe Vardaman**

248. **Joe Ray Hinds** (Tommy Gene Hinds, Laura Louise Woodbury, John Milton, David, Daniel)

He had the following children:

    422 F   i. **Cheyenne Hinds** .

    423 F   ii. **Belladonna Hinds** .

249. **Terrie L Hinds** (Tommy Gene Hinds, Laura Louise Woodbury, John Milton, David, Daniel)

Terrie married **Brad J Perry** on 28 Feb 1994.

They had the following children:

    424 M   i. **Jacob Perry**

    425 M   ii. **Bradley Perry**

    426 F   iii. **Elizabeth Perry**

    427 F   iv. **Liza Perry**

250. **Tommy Gene Hinds** (Tommy Gene Hinds, Laura Louise Woodbury, John Milton, David, Daniel)

Tommy married (1) **Angela Christine Rink** daughter of Samuel Rink and Patricia K. Rink on 21 May 2002 in Bunker Hill, Miami, Indiana, USA. Angela was born in Indiana.

Tommy married (2) **Misty** .

They had the following children:

    428 F   i. **Diana Rae Hinds** .

251. **Karrie Lynn Hinds** (Tommy Gene Hinds, Laura Louise Woodbury, John Milton, David, Daniel)

She had the following children:

    429 M   i. **Waylon Hunter Clary**

    430 F   ii. **Amber Jean Cross**

    431 F   iii. **Anastasia Chevelle Cross**

252. **Richard Mannon** (Tommy Gene Hinds, Laura Louise Woodbury, John Milton, David, Daniel)

Richard had the following children:

432 F   i. **Emily Kay Mannon** .

253. **Donald Mannon** (Tommy Gene Hinds, Laura Louise Woodbury, John Milton, David, Daniel) .

Donald married **Amanda Paupard** .
They had the following children:

433 F   i. **Kaylee Paupard**

434 F   ii. **Alexa Paupard**

435 F   iii. **Alyssa Paupard**

254. **Cynthia Mannon** (Tommy Gene Hinds, Laura Louise Woodbury, John Milton, David, Daniel)

She had the following children:

436 M   i. **Joshawa Friesel**

437 F   ii. **Julie Friesel**

438 M   iii. **James Mannon**

255. **James Samuel Culbreath** (Kathleen Ann Hinds, Laura Louise Woodbury, John Milton, David, Daniel)

James married **Glenda K Fuller** on 26 Nov 1994 in Stearns, Minnesota, USA.

They had the following children:

+   439 F   i. **Jami Culbreath**

440 F   ii. **Kathleen Culbreath**

256. **Merton Daniel Culbreath** (Kathleen Ann Hinds, Laura Louise Woodbury, John Milton, David, Daniel) was born in Naples, Collier, Florida, USA.

Merton married (1) **Monich** .

They had the following children:

441 M   i. **Jonathan Culbreath**

Merton married (2) **Danielle Lori Davies** . Danielle was born in Boynton

Beach, FL.

They had the following children:

442 M   ii. **James Clark Culbreath II** was born in West Palm Beach, Palm Beach, Florida, USA.

257. **Timothy Alan Culbreath** (Kathleen Ann Hinds, Laura Louise Woodbury, John Milton, David, Daniel) was born in Naples, Collier, Florida, USA.

Timothy married **Joyce Renea King** on 5 Mar 1988 in Wellburn, FL. Joyce was born in Russelville, AL.

They had the following children:

443 M   i. **Christopher Lee Culbreath** was born in Naples, Collier, Florida

+ 444 M   ii. **Justin Scott Culbreath**

445 M   iii. **Mark Alan Culbreath** was born in Toledo, Lucas, Ohio, USA.

258. **Laura Lorel Culbreath** (Kathleen Ann Hinds, Laura Louise Woodbury, John Milton, David, Daniel) was born in Naples, Collier, Florida, USA.

Laura married **Harry Walter Alderman II** son of Harry Alderman on 18 Nov 1985 in Naples, Collier, Florida, USA. Harry was born in Fort Myers, Lee, FL.

They had the following children:

446 M   i. **Randall Walter Alderman** was born in Gainesville, Alachua, FL.

447 M   ii. **Scott Neil Alderman** was born in Jacksonville, Duval, Florida, USA.
    Scott married **Bridgette Chittenden** .

448 M   iii. **David Allen Alderman** was born in Naples, Collier, Florida, USA.

262. **Mary Evelyn Coats** (Nancy Jean Hinds, Laura Louise Woodbury, John Milton, David, Daniel) was born in Tampa, Hillsborough, Florida, USA.

Mary married (1) **Roy E Casey** .

They had the following children:

+ 449 M   i. **Gregory Allan Coats**

+ 450 F   ii. **Misty Dawn Coats**

Mary married (2) **Jose Carmen Melendez** on 10 Sep 1990 in Palmyra, Harrison, Indiana, USA.

Mary married (3) **Fulgencio Perez** . Fulgencio was born in Puerto Rico.

They had the following children:

+   451 M   iii. **Billy Joe Perez**

+   452 F   iv. **Maryanne Perez**

263. **Vincent Ray Coats** (Nancy Jean Hinds, Laura Louise Woodbury, John Milton, David, Daniel) was born in Salem, Delaware, Indiana, USA.

He had the following children:

   453 M   i. **Travis Coats**

264. **James Eric Coats** (Nancy Jean Hinds, Laura Louise Woodbury, John Milton, David, Daniel) was born in Salem, Delaware, Indiana, USA.

James married (1) **Ann Louise Boyce** on 16 Dec 1989 in Beaufort, SC. Ann was born in Charleston, SC.

He had the following children:

   454 M   i. **James Eric Coats Jr** was born in Orlando, Brevard, Florida, USA.

265. **Karen Fay Coats** (Nancy Jean Hinds, Laura Louise Woodbury, John Milton, David, Daniel) was born in Tampa, Hillsborough, Florida, USA.

Karen married (1) **Allan Casey** .

They had the following children:

   455 M   i. **Michael Lynn Coats** was born in Salem, Delaware, Indiana, USA.

Karen married (2) **Thomas Edward Dudley** . Thomas was born in Indiana, USA.

They had the following children:

   456 M   ii. **Bradley Edward Dudley** was born in Salem, Delaware, Indiana, USA.

   457 F   iii. **Alisa Elaine Dudley** was born in Clewiston, FL.

Karen married (3) **Jeffery Harrell** .

Jeffery and Karen had the following children:

   458 M   iv. **Jeremy Harrell**

266. **Donna Jean Coats** (Nancy Jean Hinds, Laura Louise Woodbury, John Milton, David, Daniel) was born in Salem, Delaware, Indiana, USA.

Donna married (1) **Douglas Blaine Lee** on 21 Aug 1972 in Borden, IN.

They had the following children:

    459 F   i. **Bonnie Sue Lee** was born in Clewiston, FL.

    460 F   ii. **Michelle Kaye Lee** was born in Salem, Delaware, Indiana, USA.

    461 F   iii. **Karen Ann Lee** was born in Borden, IN.

Donna married (2) **Michael Etheridge Day** on 10 Oct 1984 in Albany, GA.

267. **Freeman Lloyd Coats** (Nancy Jean Hinds, Laura Louise Woodbury, John Milton, David, Daniel) was born in Tampa, Hillsborough, Florida, USA.

Freeman married **Shirley Washam** on 1 Sep 1990 in Pekin, Washington, Indiana, USA. Shirley was born in Ohio.

They had the following children:

+   462 F   i. **Jennifer Coats**

+   463 M   ii. **Steven Coats**

268. **Debra Sue Morris** (Patsy Louise Hinds, Laura Louise Woodbury, John Milton, David, Daniel) was born in Fort Benning, GA.

Debra married (1) **Larry L. Sims** in 1969. Larry was born in Hogansville, Troup, Georgia, USA.

They had the following children:

    464 M   i. **Jerry L. Sims** was born in Fort Myers, Lee, FL.

    465 F   ii. **Tammy L. Sims** was born in Punta Gorda, Charlotte, Florida, USA.

+   466 M   iii. **Larry L. Sims**

+   467 M   iv. **Barry L. Sims**

Debra married (2) **Roy F. Curry** on 6 Dec 1982.

269. **Pamela Louise Morris** (Patsy Louise Hinds, Laura Louise Woodbury, John Milton, David, Daniel).

Pamela married **James Eugene Lavelle** on 11 Aug 1971 in Lee, Florida.

They had the following children:

468 F   i. **Sherry Lavelle** .

270. **Paul Sonny Morris** (Patsy Louise Hinds, Laura Louise Woodbury, John Milton, David, Daniel)

Paul married **Denise Miller** in 1970.

They had the following children:

469 F   i. **Mariah G Morris** .

470 M   ii. **Paul F Morris**

471 F   iii. **Valerie Morris** .

272. **Robert McKinney** (Patsy Louise Hinds, Laura Louise Woodbury, John Milton, David, Daniel)

He had the following children:

472 M   i. **Michael McKinney** .

473 M   ii. **Bobby Lee McKinney** .

474 M   iii. **Robbie McKinney** .

475 M   iv. **Danial McKinney** .

273. **Ricky Eugene Mckinney** (Patsy Louise Hinds, Laura Louise Woodbury, John Milton, David, Daniel)

Ricky married **Kathy Ileen Dinehart** daughter of Leslie L. Dinehart and Margaret Bergman on 19 Aug 1977 in Lee, Florida. Kathy was born on 3 Sep 1958. She died on 14 Sep 2000 in S&S Memorial Hospital,Penn Yan,NY.

They had the following children:

476 M   i. **Ricky Alan McKinney Jr.** .

477 F   ii. **Misty Dawn McKinney** .

274. **Sherry Hinds** (Jerry Eugene Hinds, Laura Louise Woodbury, John Milton, David, Daniel)

She had the following children:

478 F   i. **Bobby Hinds**

+   479 F   ii. **Darlene Hinds**

+   480 F   iii. **Charlene Lynn Hinds**

276. **Wanda Kay Lyon** (Sandra Sue Hinds, Laura Louise Woodbury, John Milton, David, Daniel) was born in Naples, Collier, Florida, USA.

Wanda married (1) **Kim Allen** son of William Benjamin Allen on 19 Aug 1983 in Naples, Collier, Florida, USA. Kim was born in Bath, Steuben, NY.

Wanda married (2) **Jackie Lee Loving** .

They had the following children:

+   481 M   i. **Daniel Lee Allen**

+   482 M   ii. **Jennifer Lynn Allen**

277. **Randall Kelvin Lyon** (Sandra Sue Hinds, Laura Louise Woodbury, John Milton, David, Daniel) was born on 2 Sep 1959 in Naples, Collier, Florida, USA.

Randall married (1) **Alene Wilhelmina Lynk** on 23 Apr 1980 in Naples, Collier, Florida, United States of America.

Randall married (2) **Lisa Lynn Epperson** daughter of James O Epperson and Jane Estes on 20 Jun 1997 in Naples, Collier, Florida, USA. Lisa was born in Winchester, Clark, Kentucky, USA.

Randall adopted Jacqulyn

+ 483   F   i.   **Jacqulyn Renae Cheri Lyon** was born on 14 Dec 1986.

Randall married (3) **Rhonda Lynn Crouch** daughter of James Rudolph Crouch and Margaret Evans on 10 Aug 2001 in Collier, Florida. Rhonda was born in East St. Louis, St. Clair, IL.

278. **Donald Ray Lyon** (Sandra Sue Hinds, Laura Louise Woodbury, John Milton, David, Daniel) was born in Bowling Green, OH.

Donald married **Dawn Annette Scott** daughter of Andrew Mclachlan Scott and Reva Van Hoose on 15 Nov 1976 in Naples, Collier, Florida, USA. Dawn was born in Los Angeles, California, USA.

They had the following children:

484 M   i. **Donald Ray Lyon** was born in Naples, Collier, Florida, USA.

485 F   ii. **Amy Sue Lyon** was born in Naples, Collier, Florida, USA.

280. **Richard Hinds Jr** (Richard Leroy Hinds, Laura Louise Woodbury, John Milton, David, Daniel)

Richard married (1) **Lisa Bramlett** .

They had the following children:

 486 M i. **Kyle Richard Hinds**

 487 F ii. **Mandi Megan Hinds**

 488 F iii. **Leila Hinds**
       Leila married **Jeff Reaves** on 5 Jul 2016.

Richard married (2) **Sheila Baker** daughter of Baker.

281. **Phyllis Hinds** (Richard Leroy Hinds, Laura Louise Woodbury, John Milton, David, Daniel).

Phyllis married **Jim Wenrich** .

They had the following children:

 489 M i. **Tyler Wenrich** .

 490 M ii. **Travis Wenrich** .

290. **Christina Marie Rogers** (Judy Ann Rahm, Nola Mae Woodbury, John Milton, David, Daniel)

Christina married **Jeff Leichty** .

They had the following children:

 491 M i. **Robbie Leichty** .

 492 M ii. **Joshua Leichty** .

 493 M iii. **Jacob Leichty** .

 494 F iv. **Michelle Leichty** .

 495 M v. **Steven Rogers** .

 496 M vi. **Michael Rogers** .

 497 M vii. **Christopher Leichty** .

293. **Luann Marie Rahm** (Edward J. Rahm, Nola Mae Woodbury, John Milton, David, Daniel)

Luann married (1) **Tim Gibson** .

They had the following children:

    498 F   i. **Jessica Gibson** .

    499 F   ii. **Amanda Gibson** .

Luann married (2) **Gary Cole** .

They had the following children:

    500 F   iii. **Marissa Cole** .

295. **Larry D. Musser** (Edith Woodbury, Cecil Allen, John Milton, David, Daniel).

He had the following children:

    501 M   i. **Larry M. Musser II** .

    502 F   ii. **Brandy Musser** .

    503 F   iii. **Heather Musser** .

    504 M   iv. **Jeffery Musser** .

    505 F   v. **Melissa Musser** .

Larry married (2) **Donna Stucky** .

Larry married (3) **Renea Meyers** .

296. **Gary D. Musser** (Edith Woodbury, Cecil Allen, John Milton, David, Daniel)

He had the following children:

    506 F   i. **Naissa Musser** .

    507 M   ii. **Michael Musser** .

    508 M   iii. **Gary Musser** .

Gary married (2) **Pamella J Williams** on 5 Apr 1975.

Gary married (3) **Donna Plair** .

297. **Dale A. Musser** (Edith Woodbury, Cecil Allen, John Milton, David, Daniel).

Dale married **Gerri** .

They had the following children:

    509 M   i. **Brian Musser** .

    510 M   ii. **James Musser** .

298. **Robert E. Musser** (Edith Woodbury, Cecil Allen, John Milton, David, Daniel) was born in 1953. He was buried in Ottawa Hills, Lucas County, Ohio, USA.

Robert married **Teresa** .

They had the following children:

    511 F   i. **Jennifer Musser** .

    512 F   ii. **Laura Musser** .

    513 F   iii. **Julie Musser** .

299. **Larry Michael Shanaway** (Louis Leander Shanaway, Maude Florence Woodbury, John Milton, David, Daniel)

Larry married **Jo Ann Robinson** on 24 Aug 1972 in Lee, Florida.

They had the following children:

    514 F   i. **Jessica Stephen Shanaway** .

    515 M   ii. **Larry Michael Shanaway** .

    516 F   iii. **Donna Jean Shanaway** .

300. **Dennis Paul Shanaway** (Louis Leander Shanaway, Maude Florence Woodbury, John Milton, David, Daniel).

Dennis married **Bessie Myrtle Dees** on 25 Jul 1980 in Orange, Florida.

They had the following children:

    517 M   i. **Daniel Shanaway** .

    518 M   ii. **Brad Shanaway** .

    519 F   iii. **Brandy Shanaway** .

301. **Leanne Marie Shanaway** (Louis Leander Shanaway, Maude Florence Woodbury, John Milton, David, Daniel).

Leanne married **Michael Wayne Sprague** on 29 Feb 1980 in Broward, Florida.

They had the following children:

    520 F   i. **Carrie Ann Sprague** .

    521 M   ii. **Richard Louis Sprague** .

302. **Karen Lynn Shanaway** (Louis Leander Shanaway, Maude Florence Woodbury, John Milton, David, Daniel).

Karen married **Phillip Randall Winegardner** in Apr 1965 in Lee, Florida.

They had the following children:

    522 F   i. **Carolyn Marie Winegardner** .

303. **James Marvin Shanaway** (Louis Leander Shanaway, Maude Florence Woodbury, John Milton, David, Daniel)

He had the following children:

    523 M   i. **Brian Dillon** .

304. **Barbara Jean Shanaway** (Louis Leander Shanaway, Maude Florence Woodbury, John Milton, David, Daniel) was born on 29 Mar 1942 in Toledo, Lucas, Ohio, USA. She died on 4 Mar 1996 in Virginia Beach, Princess Anne, Virginia, USA.

Barbara married (1) **Paul David Rokicki** in Feb 1960 in Lee, Florida. Paul was born on 30 Jul 1938 in Ohio. He died on 12 Aug 2010.

They had the following children:

+   524 F   i. **Andrea Marie Rokicki**

Barbara married (2) **Richard Paul Zimmerman** on 24 Nov 1970 in Lee, Florida.

They had the following children:

    525 F   ii. **Melissa Dawn Zimmerman** .

    526 M   iii. **Gregory Thomas Zimmerman** .

Barbara had the following children:

    527 F   iv. **Michelle Denise Martin** .

305. **David Louis Shanaway** (Louis Leander Shanaway, Maude Florence Woodbury, John Milton, David, Daniel) was born on 30 May 1947 in Toledo, Lucas, Ohio, USA. He died on 9 Jan 1995 in Orlando, Orange, Florida, USA.

David married (1) **Jennie Belinda Watkins**

They had the following children:

528 M   i. **Brian Louis Shanaway** .

David had the following children:

529 M   ii. **Elvan Louis Norman** .

530 F   iii. **Mary-Leigh Victoria Norman** .

310. **Luann Ruth Woodbury** (John Louis, Herman Roy, John Milton, David, Daniel) was born on 26 Jul 1943 in Toledo, Lucas, Ohio, USA. She died on 22 Jan 2001.

Luann married (1) **William Davis** .

They had the following children:

+   531 M   i. **Terry Lee Woodbury**

Luann married (2) **George Lee Shrewsberry Jr** on 13 May 1959.

They had the following children:

+   532 F   ii. **Vivian Kay Shrewsberry**

Luann married (3) **Rafael Cayabyab Velasquez** on 3 Jul 1961 in Rockledge, Brevard, Florida, USA. Rafael was born on 19 Dec 1931 in Tarlac, Philippines. He died on 30 Mar 2012 in Rockledge, Brevard County, Florida, USA. He was buried in Rockledge, Brevard County, Florida, USA.

They had the following children:

+   533 F   iii. **Angela M. Velasquez**

534 M   iv. **Alexander Joseph Velasquez** was born in Patrick AFB, Brevard, FL.

+   535 M   v. **Gregorio Woodbury Velasquez**

312. **Jimmie Allen Woodbury** (John Louis, Herman Roy, John Milton, David, Daniel) was born in Swanton, Fulton, Ohio, USA.

Jimmie married **Marion Ruth Goethe** on 28 May 1966 in New Smyrna Beach, Volusia, Florida, USA. Marion was born in Jacksonville, Duval, Florida, USA.

They had the following children:

536 M   i. **Jay Montgomery Woodbury** was born in Wurzburg, Bayern, Germany.

537 M   ii. **Timothy Paul Woodbury** was born in New Smyrna Beach, Volusia, Florida, USA.

538 F   iii. **Amanda Florence Woodbury** was born in New Smyrna Beach, Volusia, Florida, USA.

539 M   iv. **John William Woodbury** was born in New Smyrna Beach, Volusia, Florida, USA.

540 M   v. **Stephen Allen Woodbury** was born on 21 May 1967 in New Smyrna Beach, Volusia, Florida, USA. He died on 22 May 1967.

541 F   vi. **Jennifer Sue Woodbury** was born on 16 Mar 1970 in Ft. Stewart, GA. She died on 16 Mar 1970 in Georgia.

542 F   vii. **Pamela Lynn Woodbury** was born on 16 Mar 1970 in Ft. Stewart, GA. She died on 16 Mar 1970.

313. **Ronald Gene Woodbury** (John Louis, Herman Roy, John Milton, David, Daniel) was born in Toledo, Lucas, Ohio, USA.

Ronald married **Charlotte Ann Ogden** on 19 Sep 1964 in Bell, CA.

They had the following children:

543 F   i. **Rene Carla Woodbury** was born on 30 Dec 1973 in Charlotte, NC. She died on 16 Nov 1980 in Charlotte, Mecklenburg, North Carolina, USA.

\+   544 M   ii. **Randy Lee Woodbury**

\+   545 M   iii. **Rodney Gene Woodbury**

314. **William Ray Woodbury** (John Louis, Herman Roy, John Milton, David, Daniel) was born on 29 Mar 1936 in Toledo, Lucas, Ohio, United States. He died on 27 Oct 1994 in Ariel, Cowlitz, Washington, United States of America.

William married **Violet Dean Cabe** on 13 Oct 1956.

William and Violet had the following children:

546 F   i. **Connie Jean Woodbury**

547 F   ii. **Brenda Lee Woodbury**

548 F   iii. **Darlene Ruthann Woodbury**

Darlene married **Wade Hampton Walker** on 11 Nov 1977 in Brevard, Florida.

549 F   iv. **Dorothy Woodbury**

550 M   v. **William Ray Woodbury Jr** was born in San Diego, California.

315. **Jack Leroy Woodbury** (John Louis, Herman Roy, John Milton, David, Daniel) was born in Toledo, Lucas, Ohio, USA.

Jack married **Norma Jean Griffin** on 6 Jul 1957 in Los Angeles, California, USA. Norma was born about 1937.

They had the following children:

551 F   i. **Katherin A Woodbury** was born in Los Angeles, California.

552 M   ii. **Michael S Woodbury** was born in Orange, California.

553 F   iii. **Deborah K Woodbury** was born in Los Angeles, California.

554 M   iv. **Paul A Woodbury** was born in Los Angeles, California.

318. **Darlene Joyce Woodbury** (Herman William, Herman Roy, John Milton, David, Daniel) was born in Toledo, Lucas, Ohio, USA.

Darlene married (1) **Patrick Clare O'Leary** on 26 Dec 1956 in Toledo, Lucas, Ohio, USA. Patrick was born in Toledo, Lucas, Ohio, USA.

They had the following children:

+   555 F   i. **Kelly Ann O'Leary**

+   556 M   ii. **Gregory Allen O'Leary**

+   557 F   iii. **Shannon Marie O'Leary**

+   558 F   iv. **Shelly Kaye O'Leary**

Darlene married (2) **Arthur L. Dudley** in 1965.

They had the following children:

+   559 F   v. **Dione Dudley**

+   560 F   vi. **Dawn Dudley**

320. **Loretta Kay Woodbury** (Ralph William, Harry Fay, John Milton, David, Daniel)

Loretta married **Stoddard** .

They had the following children:

561 F   i.   **Rachel Stoddard** .
Rachel married **Driver** .

323. **Thomas R. Woodbury** (Raymond O., Harry Fay, John Milton, David, Daniel).

Thomas married **Anna Clark** .

They had the following children:

562 F   i.   **Cara Woodbury** .

563 F   ii.   **Rhiannon Woodbury** .

564 F   iii.   **Laurena Woodbury** .

324. **Daniel W. Woodbury** (Harry Fay, Harry Fay, John Milton, David, Daniel)

Daniel married **Erlina K. Van Norman** .

They had the following children:

565 F   i.   **Melissa Woodbury** .

566 F   ii.   **Christina Woodbury** .

567 F   iii.   **Debra Woodbury** .

329. **Robert Beaty** (Dorothy Houck, Iva Irene May Queen Woodbury, John Milton, David, Daniel).

Robert married **Rosie** .

They had the following children:

568 F   i.   **Bobby Reb Beaty** .

569 F   ii.   **Summer Beaty** .

570 F   iii.   **Shelby Beaty** .

332. **Roland Beaty** (Dorothy Houck, Iva Irene May Queen Woodbury, John Milton, David, Daniel) was born on 5 Feb 1944. He died on 29 Mar 2007 in Toledo, Lucas, Ohio, United States of America.
Roland married **Marilyn J** .

They had the following children:

571 F   i.   **Sabrine M Beaty**

Sabrine married **Robert L Mackay** on 11 Apr 1992.

572 M   ii.   **Jerry Beaty** .
                Jerry married **Patricia** .

573 F   iii.   **Dorothy Beaty** .
                Dorothy married **Joseph Vardaman** .

574 F   iv.   **Marilyn Beaty** .
                Marilyn married **Nelson Foley** .

351. **Bernard Aubry Du Shane** (Tommie Milton Ray Osenbaugh, Iva Irene May Queen Woodbury, John Milton, David, Daniel) was born on 4 Nov 1947 in Toledo, Lucas, Ohio, United States. He died on 14 Jan 1988 in Kalamazoo, Kalamazoo, Michigan. He was buried in Perrysburg, Wood County, Ohio, USA.

He had the following children:

575 M   i.   **Bernie Du Shane** .

576 F   ii.   **Michelle Du Shane** .

577 M   iii.   **Robert A Du Shane** .
                Robert married **Nicole** .

578 M   iv.   **Allen Du Shane** .

359. **Harry Osenbaugh** (Zenith Charles Osenbaugh, Iva Irene May Queen Woodbury, John Milton, David, Daniel).

Harry married **Ann** .

They had the following children:

579 M   i.   **Harry Osenbaugh Jr.** .

580 F   ii.   **Ashley Nicole Osenbaugh** .

362. **Judy Elaine Osenbaugh** (Zenith Charles Osenbaugh, Iva Irene May Queen Woodbury, John Milton, David, Daniel).

Judy married **Craig Rappert** .

Craig and Judy had the following children:

581 M   i.   **Mason Rappert** .

582 M   ii.   **Chandler Rappert** .

583 M   iii.   **Kamren Rappert** .

363. **Robert Wayne Osenbaugh** (Zenith Charles Osenbaugh, Iva Irene May Queen Woodbury, John Milton, David, Daniel).

Robert married **Robin** .

They had the following children:

584 F   i. **Lalena Osenbaugh** .

585 M   ii. **Wayne Jeremy Osenbaugh** .

364. **Lori Brown** (Bonnie Osenbaugh, Iva Irene May Queen Woodbury, John Milton, David, Daniel).

Lori married (1) **Kenneth Mason** .

They had the following children:

586 M   i. **James Mason** .

587 F   ii. **Penny Mason** .

588 M   iii. **Kenneth Mason Jr.** .

Lori married (2) **Ray Osenbaugh** .

365. **Jeanna Brown** (Bonnie Osenbaugh, Iva Irene May Queen Woodbury, John Milton, David, Daniel).

Jeanna married **Steven Gomer** .

They had the following children:

589 F   i. **Dawn Gomer** .

590 M   ii. **Phillip Gomer** .

591 F   iii. **Carrie Gomer** .

592 F   iv. **Michelle Gomer** .

367. **Bonita Brown** (Bonnie Osenbaugh, Iva Irene May Queen Woodbury, John Milton, David, Daniel).
Bonita married **Daniel Welsh** .

They had the following children:

593 F   i. **Danette Welsh** .

594 F   ii. **Darlene Welsh** .

380. **David A. Woodbury** (Alvin L., Iva Irene May Queen, John Milton, David, Daniel).

David married (1) **Kay Hankens** .

David married (2) **Norma Coffelt** .

He had the following children:

595 F   i. **Carolyn Woodbury** .

596 M   ii. **David Adam Woodbury** .

597 M   iii. **David Alvin Woodbury** .

598 M   iv. **Alan Ray Woodbury** .

Seventh Generation

408. **Jessie Daniel Cass** (Debbie Sue Hinds, Tommy Gene Hinds, Laura Louise Woodbury, John Milton, David, Daniel)

Jessie married (1) **Karen Cooper** .

They had the following children:

599 M   i. **Aiden James Cass** was born in Riverside, California.

Jessie married (2) **Megan Renee Cullars** .

They had the following children:

600 F   ii. **Karlee Dee Cass** was born on 10 Apr 2014. She died on 23 Jul 2015.

601 F   iii. **Heidi Iris Cass**

602 F   iv. **Isabella ReLyn Cass**

603 F   v. **Emma Loretta Cass**

411. **Brittany Lee Hinds** (Marjorie Ann Hinds, Tommy Gene Hinds, Laura Louise Woodbury, John Milton, David, Daniel)

She had the following children:

604 M   i. **Dylan Jeffery Hinds**

413. **Samantha Roberts** (Mary Hinds, Tommy Gene Hinds, Laura Louise Woodbury, John Milton, David, Daniel)

She had the following children:

605 F   i. **Gia Roberts** .

419. **Shawna Marie Vardaman** (Diana Hinds, Tommy Gene Hinds, Laura Louise Woodbury, John Milton, David, Daniel)

Shawna married **Tommy Lee Falkenburg** .

They had the following children:

606 F   i. **MaKenna Mai Falkenburg**

439. **Jami Culbreath** (James Samuel Culbreath, Kathleen Ann Hinds, Laura Louise Woodbury, John Milton, David, Daniel)

Jami married **Anthony Frost** .

They had the following children:

607 F   i. **Alayna Frost** .

608 M   ii. **David Frost** .

609 F   iii. **Chasity Frost** .

444. **Justin Scott Culbreath** (Timothy Alan Culbreath, Kathleen Ann Hinds, Laura Louise Woodbury, John Milton, David, Daniel) was born in Toledo, Lucas, Ohio, USA.

Justin married **Sarah** .

They had the following children:

610 M   i. **Ian Scott Culbreath**

449. **Gregory Allan Coats** (Mary Evelyn Coats, Nancy Jean Hinds, Laura Louise Woodbury, John Milton, David, Daniel) was born in Clewiston, FL.

Gregory married (1) **Kelly Bolen** .

They had the following children:

611 F   i. **Taylor Bolen** .

Gregory married (2) **Angela Caudill** .

They had the following children:

    612 F   ii. **Nancy Coats** .

    613 F   iii. **Jorydon Coats** .

    614 F   iv. **Autumn Coats** .

    615 M   v. **Brandon Coats** .

Gregory married (3) **Danielle Keen** .

They had the following children:

    616 F   vi. **Sofia Coats** .

450. **Misty Dawn Coats** (Mary Evelyn Coats, Nancy Jean Hinds, Laura Louise Woodbury, John Milton, David, Daniel) was born in Salem, Delaware, Indiana, USA.

Misty married (1) **Keith D. Payne** son of Robert and Michelle on 30 Apr 1994 in Depauw, Harrison, Indiana, USA. Keith was born in KENTUCKY.

They had the following children:

    617 F   i. **Courtney Payne** .

+   618 M   ii. **Justin Payne** .

    619 M   iii. **Nicholas Payne** .
             Nicholas married **Kayla Guinn** .

Misty married (2) **Michael Long** .

They had the following children:

+   620 M   iv. **Michael Long** .

451. **Billy Joe Perez** (Mary Evelyn Coats, Nancy Jean Hinds, Laura Louise Woodbury, John Milton, David, Daniel) was born in Clewiston, FL.

Billy married (1) **Melissa DeHoney** .

They had the following children:

    621 M   i. **Joseph Dehoney** .

Billy married (2) **Dana W** .

They had the following children:

   622 M   ii. **Waylon Perez** .

   623 M   iii. **Wyatt Perez** .

452. **Maryanne Perez** (Mary Evelyn Coats, Nancy Jean Hinds, Laura Louise Woodbury, John Milton, David, Daniel) was born in Clewiston, FL.

Maryanne married (1) **Luis A. Granados** on 1 Jul 1998 in Corydon, Harrison, Indiana, USA. Luis was born in El Savador.

They had the following children:

   624 F   i. **Mikayla Granados** .

Maryanne married (2) **Markeith Pope** .

They had the following children:

   625 F   ii. **Mary Bethe Granados** .

Maryanne married (3) **Juan Lopez** .

Juan and Maryanne had the following children:

   626 F   iii. **Katherin Cernia Perez** .

Maryanne married (4) **Jose Banilla** .

They had the following children:

   627 M   iv. **Jonathan Perez** .

Maryanne married (5) **Miguel Chavez** on 14 Jun 2010 in Dubois, Indiana, USA.

They had the following children:

   628 M   v. **Edward Chavez** .

   629 F   vi. **Elizabeth Chavez** .

   630 M vii. **Miguel Chavez** .

462. **Jennifer Coats** (Freeman Lloyd Coats, Nancy Jean Hinds, Laura Louise Woodbury, John Milton, David, Daniel).

Jennifer married **Mark Winn** .

They had the following children:

   631 M   i. **Eli Winn**

463. **Steven Coats** (Freeman Lloyd Coats, Nancy Jean Hinds, Laura Louise Woodbury, John Milton, David, Daniel)

Steven married **Jayme** .

They had the following children:

   632 F   i. **Emily Coats** .

   633 M   ii. **Blake Coats** .

   634 F   iii. **Mackinze Coats** .

466. **Larry L. Sims** (Debra Sue Morris, Patsy Louise Hinds, Laura Louise Woodbury, John Milton, David, Daniel) was born in Fort Myers, Lee, FL.

Larry married **Renee Rich** .

They had the following children:

   635 F   i. **Samantha Blair Sims**

   636 M   ii. **Larry L. Sims**

467. **Barry L. Sims** (Debra Sue Morris, Patsy Louise Hinds, Laura Louise Woodbury, John Milton, David, Daniel) was born in Fort Myers, Lee, FL.

Barry married **Lisa Padrone** .

They had the following children:

   637 F   i. **Brittney L. Sims**

479. **Darlene Hinds** (Sherry Hinds, Jerry Eugene Hinds, Laura Louise Woodbury, John Milton, David, Daniel)

She had the following children:

   638 F   i. **Gracie Lynn Hinds** .

480. **Charlene Lynn Hinds** (Sherry Hinds, Jerry Eugene Hinds, Laura Louise

Woodbury, John Milton, David, Daniel)

Charlene married **Joseph Wayne Williams.**
They had the following children:

    639 M   i. **Brandon Lee Eugene Williams**

    640 F   ii. **Kara Ann Williams**

481. **Daniel Lee Allen** (Wanda Kay Lyon, Sandra Sue Hinds, Laura Louise Woodbury, John Milton, David, Daniel) was born in Naples, Collier, Florida, USA.

He had the following children:

    641 M   i. **Alex Colton Allen** was born in Greenville, SC.

    642 M   ii. **Aiden Wyatt Allen** was born in Greenville, SC.

    643 F   iii. **Riley Jo Allen** was born in Easley, SC.

482. **Jennifer Lynn Allen** (Wanda Kay Lyon, Sandra Sue Hinds, Laura Louise Woodbury, John Milton, David, Daniel) was born in Naples, Collier, Florida, USA.

He had the following children:

    644 F   i. **Adalyn Kae Allen** was born in Greenville, SC.

    645 M   ii. **Robert Landyn Gonzalez** was born in Greenville, SC.

    646 M   iii. **Andrew Shane Allen** was born in Greenville, SC.

483. **Jacqulyn Renae Cheri Lyon** (Randall Kelvin Lyon, Sandra Sue Hinds, Laura Louise Woodbury, John Milton, David, Daniel) was born in Lexington, Fayette County, KY.

Jacqulyn married **Kelan R Thompson** son of Neal Thompson and Antonine on 30 Nov 2013.

They had the following children:

    647 F   i. **Mira Eden Thompson** was born in Oshkosh, Winnebago, Wisconsin, USA.

524. **Andrea Marie Rokicki** (Barbara Jean Shanaway, Louis Leander Shanaway, Maude Florence Woodbury, John Milton, David, Daniel) was born in Fort Myers, FL.

Andrea married **Hans Joachim Matheis** son of Raimund Hans Matheis. Hans was born on 13 Oct 1960 in Neunkirchen, Saarland, Germany. He died on 13 Feb 2007 in Watertown, Jefferson, New York, USA.

They had the following children:

    648 M   i. **Nicholas Charles Matheis** was born in Orlando, Orange County, Florida, USA.

    649 M   ii. **Brandon Eric Matheis** was born in Portsmouth, Independent Cities, Virginia, USA.

    650 M   iii. **Christopher Joachim Matheis** was born in Yuma, Arizona, USA.

531. **Terry Lee Woodbury** (Luann Ruth Woodbury, John Louis, Herman Roy, John Milton, David, Daniel) was born in Rockledge, Brevard, Florida, USA.

Terry married **Rita Carol Schofield** on 29 Apr 1977 in Pensacola, Escambia, Florida, USA.

They had the following children:

    651 F   i. **Stephanie Lynn Woodbury** was born in Pensacola, Escambia, Florida, USA.

    652 M   ii. **Joshua Shane Woodbury** was born in Pensacola, Escambia, Florida, USA.

532. **Vivian Kay Shrewsberry** (Luann Ruth Woodbury, John Louis, Herman Roy, John Milton, David, Daniel) was born in Rockledge, Brevard, Florida, USA.

Vivian married (1) **John Milton Norton** on 18 Jul 1980 in Brevard, Florida.

Vivian married (2) **Chris Wesley** .

Vivian married (3) **Noel Remillard** .

Vivian married (4) **David Frank Whitwell** on 12 Feb 1982 in Cocoa, FL. David was born in Humbolt, Tenn.

They had the following children:

    653 F   i. **Brandi Nichole Whitwell** was born in Rockledge, Brevard, Florida, USA.

    654 M   ii. **Christopher Scott Whitwell** was born in Cocoa Beach, FL.

533. **Angela M. Velasquez** (Luann Ruth Woodbury, John Louis, Herman Roy, John Milton, David, Daniel) was born in Athens, Clarke, GA.

Angela married **Gregory Allen O'Leary** son of Patrick Clare O'Leary and Darlene Joyce Woodbury on 23 Jan 1987.

They had the following children:

655 F   i.   **Jessica Lynn O'Leary** was born in Toledo, Lucas, Ohio, USA.

656 M   ii.   **Gregory Allen O'Leary Jr** was born in Rockledge, Brevard, Florida, USA.

535. **Gregorio Woodbury Velasquez** (Luann Ruth Woodbury, John Louis, Herman Roy, John Milton, David, Daniel) was born in Patrick AFB, Brevard, FL.

Gregorio married **Dawn** .

They had the following children:

657 F   i.   **Megan Rae Southwood** was born in OH.

544. **Randy Lee Woodbury** (Ronald Gene, John Louis, Herman Roy, John Milton, David, Daniel)

He had the following children:

658 M   i.   **Randall T Woodbury** .

545. **Rodney Gene Woodbury** (Ronald Gene, John Louis, Herman Roy, John Milton, David, Daniel) was born in Los Angeles, California.

Rodney married (1) **Leona Padgett Broome** .

Rodney and Leona had the following children:

659 M   i.   **Rodney Woodbury** .

Rodney married (2) **Anna Berrier** .

555. **Kelly Ann O'Leary** (Darlene Joyce Woodbury, Herman William, Herman Roy, John Milton, David, Daniel) was born in Toledo, Lucas, Ohio, USA.

She had the following children:

660 F   i.   **Penny O'Leary** .

661 M   ii.   **Patrick O'Leary** .

556. **Gregory Allen O'Leary** (Darlene Joyce Woodbury, Herman William, Herman Roy, John Milton, David, Daniel)

Gregory married **Angela M. Velasquez** daughter of Rafael Cayabyab Velasquez and Luann Ruth Woodbury on 23 Jan 1987. Angela was born on in Athens, Clarke, GA.

They had the following children:

662 F   i.   Jessica Lynn O'Leary (#655)

663 M   ii.   Gregory Allen O'Leary Jr (#656)

557. **Shannon Marie O'Leary** (Darlene Joyce Woodbury, Herman William, Herman Roy, John Milton, David, Daniel) was born in Toledo, Lucas, Ohio, USA.

Shannon married **Clifford Brimmer** .

They had the following children:

664 M   i.   **Shawn Brimmer** .

665 M   ii.   **Josh Brimmer** .

+   666 F   iii.   **Colleen Brimmer** .

667 F   iv.   **Jolleen Brimmer** .

558. **Shelly Kaye O'Leary** (Darlene Joyce Woodbury, Herman William, Herman Roy, John Milton, David, Daniel) was born in Toledo, Lucas, Ohio, USA.

Shelly married **Russell Byram** .

Russell and Shelly had the following children:

668 F   i.   **Michelle Byram** .

669 F   ii.   **Stacy Byram** .

559. **Dione Dudley** (Darlene Joyce Woodbury, Herman William, Herman Roy, John Milton, David, Daniel)

Dione married **Jeff Rollins** .

They had the following children:

670 M   i.   **Aaron Rollins** .

671 F   ii.   **Amanda Rollins** .

672 M   iii.   **Anthony Rollins** .

560. **Dawn Dudley** (Darlene Joyce Woodbury, Herman William, Herman Roy, John Milton, David, Daniel)

Dawn married **Larry Streets** on 15 Aug 1992.

They had the following children:

673 F   i.   **Brandon Streets** .

674 F   ii. **Misty Streets** .

Eighth Generation

618. **Justin Payne** (Misty Dawn Coats, Mary Evelyn Coats, Nancy Jean Hinds, Laura Louise Woodbury, John Milton, David, Daniel).

Justin married **Allie Taylor** .

They had the following children:

    675 F   i. **Carmen Payne** .

    676 F   ii. **Claire Payne** .

620. **Michael Long** (Misty Dawn Coats, Mary Evelyn Coats, Nancy Jean Hinds, Laura Louise Woodbury, John Milton, David, Daniel).

Michael married **Samantha Fox** .

They had the following children:

    677 F   i. **Mia Long** .

    678 M   ii. **Mason Bowen** .

666. **Colleen Brimmer** (Shannon Marie O'Leary, Darlene Joyce Woodbury, Herman William, Herman Roy, John Milton, David, Daniel).

Colleen married **Robert Marchalewski** .

They had the following children:

    679 M   i. **Damon Lee Marchalewski**

    680 M   ii. **Robert Marchalewski Jr**

www.ingramcontent.com/pod-product-compliance
Lightning Source LLC
Chambersburg PA
CBHW072039280526
45788CB00006B/2114